The Lindbergh of Canada: The Erroll Boyd Story

maple leaf
Harry Connor
Errol Boyd
1930

by ROSS SMYTH

Published by

GENERAL STORE
PUBLISHING HOUSE

1 Main Street Burnstown, Ontario, Canada K0J 1G0
Telephone 1-800-465-6072, Fax (613) 432-7184

ISBN 1-896182-61-5
Printed and bound in Canada

The General Store Publishing House
Burnstown, Ontario, Canada

Canadian Cataloguing in Publication Data

Smyth, Ross, 1921 –
    The Lindbergh of Canada : the Erroll Boyd story

ISBN 1-896182-61-5

    1. Boyd, Erroll.   2. Air pilots – Canada – Biography.
I. Title.

TL540.B69S55 1997   629.13′092   C97-900509-4

First Printing June 1997

Acknowledgements

Many members of Erroll Boyd's family made this book possible, mainly his daughters, Mrs. Bey Hartford and Mrs. Honor Boyd Smith, and his grandson Bruce Knight. Their help in locating records and scrapbooks facilitated my research in Ottawa and Washington.

This book would not have been possible without the help of many enthusiastic members of a lively organization, the Canadian Aviation Historical Society, ranging from Canada's first national aviation museum curator, the late Ken Molson, to the collector of thousands of aviation publications, Ross Richardson.

Being a pioneer employee of Air Canada facilitated my exploratory travels ranging from Harbour Grace in Newfoundland to Canada's west coast and from the Smithsonian Institute in Washington to interviewing relatives in Pompano Beach, Florida. To the many dozens of people who assisted me, I am very grateful.

The fact that Captain Erroll Boyd was a boyhood hero of mine simplified the task.

Ross Smyth
1997

Captain Erroll Boyd (Courtesy of Boyd family)

Captain Erroll Boyd (Courtesy of Boyd family)

Foreword

When Ross Smyth invited me to write the foreword for his book, *The Lindbergh of Canada*, I recalled my first relatively routine flight over the once treacherous North Atlantic in the very early 1950s in a then luxurious TCA North Star airliner.

I knew relatively little of the aviation adventures of Erroll Boyd even after my nearly half-century association with the industry. This is a story about a great Canadian who lived most of his active life early in this century when many Canadians still retained a colonial mentality without sufficient pride in their own endeavours.

When reading this manuscript, I developed an intense admiration for Boyd's heroic 1930 achievement when, after many legal barriers, great planning and then weather delays, he flew non-stop from Newfoundland to the southwest tip of England in a five-year-old Bellanca in just over twenty-four hours to be the very first such crossing outside the much favoured summer season. Others had tried but disappeared into oblivion.

Air Canada's own early transatlantic efforts in wartime over this route confirmed its reputation as the most difficult ocean to fly because of its adverse weather and the pronounced effect of seasonal changes on flight operations. Boyd carried no radio due to its weight and limited range, but was accompanied by Harry Connor as navigator who had flown with him to Bermuda earlier that year. He was aided, particularly during the long night, by a very new instrument, the artificial horizon. Even then this skilful and cautious pilot barely made it to a very small beach in England's Scilly Isles due to a blocked fuel line.

Boyd's air adventures began in the early part of World War I when Captain John Alcock, R.N.A.S., taught him to fly before the existence of any flight training schools in Canada. Boyd chased Zeppelins and submarines before being shot down and interned in

Holland in 1915. This talented aviator pioneered with small airlines in the 1920s, and flew the first non-stop flight from New York to Haiti in 1933.

Erroll Boyd was a man in advance of his time. His aviation columns in the 1930s in Miami and Toronto publications reflected the industry's future often better than its leaders or politicians. His career spanned a time when middle-aged pilots were considered old for active flying during the hungry thirties. Without government assistance he formed the Aviation Scouts of Canada, a forerunner of the Air Cadet movement. When World War II broke out, he recruited hundreds of pilots for the war effort.

As a boy in school in Toronto, author Ross Smyth won a flight to Miami in Boyd's aviation scouts before the commencement of airline service across Canada. Employed by T.C.A. and Air Canada 1940-1977, Smyth was in the first group of flight dispatchers assigned to the airline's transatlantic region. Since his retirement he has flown a light aircraft across both Canada and the U.S.A., continuing his love affair with flying.

Contributing an important chapter to the exciting history of flight, this nostalgic book gives insights of air history in the making. It tells a story not only for aviation buffs but one that can be enjoyed by all who experience air travel today as a common occurrence.

Claude I. Taylor, O.C.
Chairman Emeritus
Air Canada

Montreal, June, 1997

Table of Contents

The Columbia, world's most famous aeroplane, twice conqueror of the Atlantic. Inset, Capt. J. Erroll Boyd.

Autographed postcard of Columbia (Courtesy of Boyd family)

1

A Forgotten Canadian Hero

IN 1940 Captain Erroll Boyd received this very short letter from his dying father:

Toronto, April 5, 1940

Dear Erroll:

For a man with some good brains you continue to sell them for a poor income. Why so silly?

Dad

This note summarized the plight of many dedicated pioneer pilots whose heroic exploits laid the groundwork for today's airlines and created headlines in the Golden Age of Flight, the period between the two great wars (1918-1939). Today, with a few exceptions like Charles Lindbergh and Amelia Earhart, their names are forgotten.

Who knows, for example, that this Canadian pilot, Erroll Boyd, was the first to prove that flight by airplane over the treacherous north Atlantic Ocean was feasible outside the summer season? It was not until World War II that this route was conquered on a regular, year-round basis.

Erroll Boyd began his flying before the Golden Age. Born in 1891, he had his first flight as a passenger in 1912 with the famous American barnstorming pilot Lincoln Beachey in a ride that ultimately decided his life career. During World War I he became one of the first Canadians to enlist in the Royal Naval Air Service that Winston

Churchill had founded in 1912. At Eastchurch in England in 1915 he received his first instruction in flying in a flimsy Wright biplane with the crude system of wing warping for lateral control. His instructor was John Alcock, later to become famous and knighted for the first non-stop transatlantic flight in 1919. Eleven years after Alcock's feat, Boyd would become the second British pilot to successfully fly from east to west across the treacherous North Atlantic Ocean.

Boyd was an early seeker of adventure. As a boy of four he dove off steamers at Owen Sound, Ontario, under the watchful eyes of his loving mother. He later won trophies for his canoeing skill. As a young man in New York he earned money performing water stunts. He also served as a test pilot on early models of untried aircraft.

Unlike earlier famous record flights, Boyd successfully flew the North Atlantic in 1930 late in the year, a dangerous time due to the much longer nights and more hazardous weather. The obstacles that Boyd and his navigator conquered provided an early indication that year-round transatlantic air service was feasible.

Boyd's flying was not his only vocation, his mother told the press when he was over the Atlantic Ocean in 1930. In his first thirty-eight years this talented Canadian was an automobile salesman, manager of a large grocery warehouse, a mail and test pilot, operations manager of an airline and a musical composer.

Erroll Boyd obviously inherited his adventurous nature from his mother, a descendant of the United Empire Loyalists, those Americans who fled the revolution to build homes in the Canadian wilderness. On the other hand, a close study of his record reveals a very competent and careful pilot. His sense of caution originated with his father, James Tower Boyd, a conservative insurance executive and descendant of Lord Erroll of Scotland. It was no accident that Erroll Boyd survived some 9,000 hours of flight in almost all types of early flying machines.

Boyd was a man who possessed the perseverance to reach his goals. Failing the vision test in the Royal Flying Corps in 1915, the persistent Boyd succeeded in joining the Royal Naval Air Service, serving in England and France. He hunted Zeppelins and submarines with crude little bombs attached to his undercarriage in the early part of the Great War. He fought this way until he was hit by German anti-aircraft fire in October 1915, and interned after landing his badly damaged ship in Holland.

Boyd entered the air war of World War I far too early to achieve a long record of military action. Honours for shooting down a large number of enemy aircraft were achieved by the heroic men like Billie Bishop, Eddie Rickenbacker and Manfred von Richthofen who came along later, mostly in 1917 and 1918.

Boyd's writings and notes at a more mature age reveal that he disliked war and killing, and at times had questioned the wisdom of the politicians and senior officers. No "yes" man, he was an intelligent, thinking individual.

Boyd's pacifism was best revealed by his friendship with the manager of Henry Ford's peace ship to Europe during World War I. Boyd later concurred with the views of Clifford Harmon, of Harmon Trophy renown, who advocated in 1929 a global peace air force, a vision today not yet realized. Captain Erroll Boyd was a man of peace in an era when peace heroes were rare and society preferred war heroes.

Almost giving up flying by instruments in mountainous Mexico in 1928, he again proved his perseverance and became probably the first Canadian aviator quite competent at "blind flying" well before the issuance of instrument ratings.

Captain Boyd was an unselfish, generous man and great humanitarian, but not a good money manager. In the depression year of 1937 he was completely broke, and a Toronto bailiff was seizing his property. The following year, without any government assistance, he had rebounded sufficiently to organize the forerunner of the air cadet movement, the Aviation Scouts of Canada, to promote aviation among youth and their elders.

A very modest man, his aviation columns in the Toronto Star Weekly and earlier in the Miami press seldom referred to his own achievements. Many of his forecasts for the future, often contrary to conventional wisdom, proved quite accurate and convinced thousands to become boosters for the development of safe and efficient air transportation. He was a man ahead of his time.

Erroll Boyd was an optimist, a romantic and a dreamer. His dreams to fly the Atlantic Ocean and to Bermuda were reported in the press as early as 1916; he made them a reality fourteen years later. He foresaw a great future for aviation even though its progress was slowed by the worldwide depression of the 1930s and the public fear of flying at that time.

Besides his obsessive love and continuing return to aviation, this man had the ability and background to be successful in any number of other fields in which he dabbled. One of the songs for which he wrote the lyrics, Dreams, became a hit on Broadway in the early 1920s. This early airman and his many acquaintances, both humble and famous, lived exciting lives in exciting times.

There were many ups and downs for these air pioneers. In the depression era their timing was not always favourable. In the aviation business of the 1930s and early 1940s, a person over forty was considered by most as being too old for flying, believed to be a young man's game. Regardless of their personal capacities the older air pioneers were too frequently considered ex-stunt men well past their prime. The growth of employment in aviation, as in most other fields, was almost at a standstill during the 1930s.

Boyd had just moved to the U.S. for better employment opportunity when World War II broke out. In spite of his yearning for peace, he immediately recognized the global threat of Hitlerism and its authoritarian principles. Unacceptable for military service, he directed hundreds of American flyers to volunteer for the Allied cause before the Japanese invasion of Pearl Harbor forced the U.S. to enter into the global conflict. His courageous activity was both intuitive and contrary to the intention of U.S. neutrality legislation.

Erroll Boyd was a man who loved life, who ate and drank well, and who enjoyed good company. On parole from internment in Holland during the First World War, he married a Broadway musical dancer in New York. The renowned Al Jolsen threw a party for the newlyweds. Their marriage produced five beautiful girls, some born in the U.S.A., some in Canada, but all baptized in Toronto. Thus Erroll Boyd typified the reality of the growing closeness of Canadian-American relations well before the free trade era.

This quintessential Canadian was not adequately recognized by Canada in the 1930s because of the country's colonial mentality and lack of national pride. His achievements will gain greater recognition with time. A citizen of both Canada and the United States, he was, in a psychological sense, a "world citizen," a lover of all humanity.

The National Air and Space Museum of the Smithsonian Institute in Washington has a large file including more than 100 pages of press clippings on Erroll Boyd. He is also recognized in Canada's Aviation Museum at Rockliffe Airport in Ottawa.

Erroll was on a first name basis with many of the key pioneers of the Golden Age of Flight, the men and women who made the marvels of modern flight possible. This, then, is not only his story but theirs also – the air pioneers of the inter-war period. This lovable Canadian, Erroll Boyd, was often dubbed the Lindbergh of Canada in the American press.

Erroll was on a first name basis with many of the key pioneers of the Golden Age of Flight, the men and women who made the marvels of modern flight possible. This, then, is not only his story but theirs also – the air pioneers of the interwar period. This lovable Canadian, Erroll Boyd, was often dubbed the Lindbergh of Canada in the American press.

2

Conquering the Atlantic

ERROLL BOYD gunned the motor of his Bellanca monoplane to full power at the extreme eastern end of the single runway at Harbour Grace, Newfoundland, but she would not budge. She was so heavily loaded with fuel that the tail skid had sunk into the rocky runway, acting as a brake. This was the inauspicious start of the first flight by a Canadian across the Atlantic Ocean, a journey that had already claimed the lives of so many airmen.

It was the early afternoon of October 9, 1930. It was only a year after the New York stock market crash and the beginning of the worldwide depression of the thirties that would slow investment in air travel. It was the beginning of a journey that would fulfil the dream and goal set by Erroll Boyd during the Great War when he had served as one of the first Canadian pilots in the Royal Naval Air Service.

Harbour Grace, a small town across Conception Bay from St. John's, was becoming famous. In the following year Wiley Post and Harold Gatty would use it as their Atlantic departure point on their record-breaking round-the-world flight of just under nine days. In 1932 Amelia Earhart would depart from here on her record solo flight to Ireland.

The departure point in no way resembled the vast modern airports of the jet age. It consisted of one narrow, sloping, unpaved runway approximately 200 feet above sea level and running almost east and west.

Behind Boyd as he attempted his takeoff was an abrupt rocky hill formation jutting up fifty feet into the air at the eastern end of the runway. The runway was about 175 feet in width and sloped at the sides. The only good portion for take-off was about 3,000 feet in length. Beyond this section was broken rock and stone. Only a take-off to the west was possible in a heavily loaded aircraft because of the rock wall at the east end.

The North Atlantic route ahead contained some of the world's worst flying weather, an added hazard for aircraft of that period, aircraft that lacked cabin pressurization, de-icing equipment and engine reliability.

There had been only four successful eastbound crossings following Lindbergh's: Clarence Chamberlain, Richard Byrd, and the team of Brock and Schlee in 1927, and Wilmer Stultz in 1928. All of these earlier flights had crossed under summer conditions, which provided the best weather and most daylight. The autumn of 1930 provided very unfavourable weather with the fast approach of winter. Boyd had obtained weather reports through E. O'Donnell of the Canadian Meteorological Service in Toronto, and, while technically out of the U.S. Weather Bureau's jurisdiction, had some cooperation from its New York expert, Dr. J.H. Kimball. The Canadian pilot and his navigator, Harry Connor, had also made arrangements through the Radio Marine Corporation in New York to have ocean liners at sea forward regular weather reports. The two airmen would carry a chart showing the position of every vessel crossing the Atlantic in both directions. Knowing each ship's respective speed would help them to check their own position.

"Easterly winds and gales had been blowing over almost the entire Atlantic for nearly three weeks," reported Harry Connor, who would accompany Howard Hughes on his record round-the-world flight eight years later. "There seemed to be no let up, and we were becoming quite discouraged. I we decided to have our ship ready for a take-off at the first sign of a decent break in the weather."

On October 7 Boyd and Connor received the first intimation of a break in the easterly gales. On October 8 they received the following weather report from Toronto:

Area of high pressure over Newfoundland extends eastward over Atlantic to about longitude thirty degrees (the halfway point), while deep depression mentioned yesterday is centered over Scotland. A shallow depression centered southeast of Newfoundland about latitude thirty three degrees longitude forty-five degrees. Conditions over Eastern Atlantic and British Isles too stormy to start today.

This report, combined with others from ships at sea, appeared to Boyd and Connor to be as favourable as they could expect at that time of the year, so they cabled Toronto for further information to verify the steamer reports.

The Canadian Meteorological Service in Toronto replied: "Have nothing further to information given to you this morning. Atlantic and European reports only received once a day. Why not await tomorrow's report?"

Deciding to wait no longer, Boyd and Connor planned a sunrise takeoff on October 9. Their plans, however, were further thwarted. They awakened early to see Harbour Grace covered with a heavy morning fog that would delay their departure until early afternoon. While aircraft normally depart into the wind to shorten the takeoff distance, Boyd and Connor would have to take off to the west with a light easterly tailwind because of the wall of rock at the eastern end of the field.

Before taking off, Boyd had made a very thorough study of the runway. He had examined the exact spot on the field where Captain John Henry Mears and his pilot, Harry Brown, had cracked up in the City of New York on take-off two months earlier on their round-the-world attempt in a Lockheed Vega. To avoid a similar fate, Boyd and Connor placed the Bellanca in the northeast corner at the east end of the runway. They planned to move diagonally at first down the runway until they expected to have good directional control after having travelled the downward-sloping 1,000 feet. Boyd described it as follows:

> After warming up the engine we buckled our belts and were ready for what I considered the most hazardous part of the flight – the first few moments which could mean the difference between life and death. We tensed as I gave the engine full throttle and waited for the first rolling movement of the heavily loaded ship. The engine roared but the ship wouldn't budge due to the heavy load, and the fact that the tail skid dug into the rocky runway, serving as a brake.

Throttling back the engine I got out of the plane and instructed several of the onlookers to push us. Returning to the cockpit I again gunned the engine, and with the help of the men who shoved, the ship started to move slowly down the runway, heading for the spot where Brown and Mears had cracked up. I had little control for the first 1,000 feet – the dragging tail skid continued to act as a brake until the tail gradually lifted from the ground. At this point I cautiously eased my right rudder pedal and the aircraft responded, slowly bearing to the right, and in short order we were rolling down the centre of the strip.

Some 3,000 feet remained as we nosed into the west with the ship slowly gaining speed, and myself gradually gaining confidence. I still dared not try to lift the plane until every foot of the strip had been used. As I approached the end, I gently eased the stick back. Feeling the plane lift, I was elated that we were now in the air. The famous little plane which had already spanned the Atlantic three years ago, again very heavily loaded, responded to the controls and we were on our way.

They had taken off in the early afternoon in Newfoundland on October 9, 1930, at 16:18Z Greenwich mean time, now known as universal time (hereafter abbreviated with a Z). As a transatlantic flight involves several time zones, this avoids the confusion of making frequent time changes, and is the time at the zero meridian running through Greenwich, England. Connor noted the take-off run took twenty-seven seconds, after which the plane headed eastbound at 600 feet.

Boyd later said:

I had hoped for an earlier start giving us the opportunity of using up at least 100 gallons of fuel before darkness which would have lightened the plane some 600 pounds making flying much easier during the long, dark hours ahead of us. With a heavy load the Bellanca tends to hunt and fall off on either wing, which would probably have sent the ship spinning into the Atlantic.

Total fuel at take-off was 460 U.S. gallons (about thirty-five hours of flying) and twenty-seven gallons of oil. These represented over half of the gross weight of 5,200 pounds. Connor's report said the gross weight included fifteen pounds of official mail and Erroll's weight of 215 pounds, somewhat heavier than in his athletic younger days!

Due to considerations of weight, no radio was carried. Radio equipment would have weighed about eighty pounds, which would have meant sacrificing thirteen gallons of fuel or about one hour of flying time. While forsaking the unreliable radio of that era, Boyd and Connor did carry the new Sperry gyro horizon to facilitate flight in cloud and during the long night. It had been installed in Montreal to be ready for its first transatlantic flight.

The fliers had declared that their attempt was intended as a scientific venture and "not a hit or miss idea." Boyd wanted to prove the feasibility of early commercial air service on the route. Dr. Kimball, the transatlantic weather expert in New York, told the press that, while the weather was not too good, he had confidence in the crew, having worked with them on their earlier record flight to Bermuda.

To stress the routine nature of the trip, Boyd and Connor were dressed in ordinary business clothes plus the customary pilot helmets. They were seated on a twenty-seven gallon oil tank, which at least kept the lower part of their bodies warm.

Connor later wrote about the flight: "Erroll did the best job in his life when he took that ship off, for I considered that the hardest part of the whole flight, and I breathed easily once more when we were in the air."

But the rest of the flight was not easy. In the middle of the ocean they were to encounter stormy weather and icing conditions requiring a considerable detour. The fuel flow from their 100-gallon reserve tank would be cut off. After nearly twenty-four hours in the air Boyd would make an emergency landing on a tiny beach on an island off the southwest tip of England with the remaining fuel tanks almost dry.

Transatlantic pioneer Charles A. Lindbergh, acting as technical consultant to Juan Trippe and Pan American Airways, would say three years later: "The North Atlantic is the most important, and also the most difficult to fly, of all the oceans crossed by the trade routes of men."

3

Reminiscences of the Young Erroll

JAMES ERROLL DUNSFORD BOYD was born in Toronto on November 22, 1891 – the beginning of an adventurous life. More than a half century later he reminisced about his early youth growing up in a moderately affluent Toronto family in the 1890s, and about the influence on him of his brother, Norman, nearly five years his senior:

> I left solid terra firma for the first time at the behest of my brother. At his direction from the age of five I was climbing to stratospheric heights of the tallest trees in search of bird eggs. Many were the falls I experienced when fragile branch tips could not bear even my slight weight and more than once the precious eggs I carried in my mouth for safe return to earth were crushed between my jaws when I slipped and fell.
>
> Norman did no tree climbing himself and I alone served as his retriever. When, after several seasons of work, the eggs I had collected were adjudged the finest juvenile exhibit in Canada, the certificate from the Canadian Ornithological Society awarding the honour brought distinctions to the Boyd home in the name of Norman only. Nor was that Tarzan period the only experience above the earth planned for me by my brother.
>
> A few years later he designed a parachute and I was elected to be his guinea pig in testing the arrangement of bed sheets and string which might bring some new honour to brother Norman. I was not wholly a dullard, and when attached to his parachute, I looked down from the barn roof, and my blood bond with the inventor failed to meet the test.

The young Erroll (Courtesy of Boyd family)

Protesting, I started to disengage myself from the
apparatus. My brother, however, was a man of action and he did
not waste time arguing. He pushed me off the roof. I know he
was disappointed when the parachute failed to function as he
had planned, and I wound up with broken ribs and contusions.

Erroll's mother, interviewed during his transatlantic flight,
recalled that overcoming obstacles had always been the specialty of
her son:

The first prize he ever won was in an obstacle race at St. Andrew's
College when he was only eight years old. "The cup is upstairs," she
explained. "Obstacles were never anything to him. When only four
years old, he could dive magnificently. At Owen Sound he would
actually dive off the steamers."

Erroll's eldest daughter Bay, born in 1918, has many childhood
memories of her grandmother's tales of Erroll's sport trophies and
mischievous adventures. "Dad as a youngster had a cranky neighbour,"
she recalls, "so he placed a dead mouse on Mr. Locksley's silver butter
dish which was under a cover outside his dining room window!"

Bey's grandmother told her of her dad's curiosity at a young age.
When he was fifteen, Erroll took his motorcycle completely apart and
then put it all back together again perfectly, working in the basement
of the family's Bedford Street home in Toronto.

The young Erroll Boyd always had an attraction for the water,
and became an expert canoeist. He competed successfully in junior
and senior canoe categories as well as in tilting and swimming.

Erroll Boyd was educated at two excellent private schools near
Toronto: Trinity College and St. Andrew's College. He was at Trinity
a short time and then at St. Andrew's from 1902 until 1909. The
school records reveal that he went to work with the Standard Bank of
Canada following graduation. J.A.D. McCurdy, Philip C. Garratt and
Jack T. Dyment were other eminent aviation personalities who
graduated from St. Andrew's College. In 1937 Boyd addressed their
Old Boys' Dinner, and many years later he was a special guest at
Trinity College.

Brother Norman Boyd was again an intermediate impresario on
Erroll's first legitimate flight. The year was 1912. Erroll, then twenty,
had a summer job in a hotel where Norman was a guest. They both
had witnessed a historic flight of the great Lincoln Beachey the year

before when the great American barnstormer had amazed throngs by flying under the International Bridge at Niagara Falls. It was the same Lincoln Beachey who, on July 12, 1906, had made the first recorded and advertised exhibition of a power-driven airship in Montreal when he rose from the grounds of Dominion Park in a machine of his own construction. Both Norman and Erroll had been introduced to the hero by their father who had several business dealings with Beachey regarding insurance.

A year later they renewed their acquaintance with Beachey, who was then flying a Curtiss hydroplane, but had not had a passenger since his arrival. As a showman Beachey knew he needed to demonstrate the safety of flying by getting a hardy individual to accompany him. Others would follow when the ice had been broken. Brother Norman instantly saw the logic of Beachey's idea, and at once volunteered his younger brother, Erroll!

Sitting in the open and clinging firmly to the struts, Erroll enjoyed the flight thoroughly, though it was only a few minutes in duration. True to Beachey's instinct, the trip resulted in a number of less cautious Canadians overcoming their natural thrift to offer payment, and Beachey was in business. That flight determined Erroll's life career and, as it reflected only minimum glory on brother Norman, from that day on Erroll was on his own.

Boyd spent most of his youth in the family home at 121 Bedford Road in Toronto. His father, James Tower Boyd, spent all his working life with Confederation Life Assurance where he rose to be general manager of agencies. His father, Erroll's grandfather, was a descendent of James Boyd, Earl of Erroll of Aberdeen, Scotland. Erroll's mother, the former Minnie Arabella Dunsford, was a descendent of a United Empire Loyalist family originally from Devon in England. The Dunsfords were early settlers in the Kawartha Lakes district of Ontario. One of them, Ann Langton, wrote a book entitled *A Gentlewoman in Upper Canada*.

Older brother Norman apparently took some pride in his younger brother's daring and, often in later years, helped Erroll through some of his more difficult financial times. Like his father before him, Norman achieved a successful business career with Confederation Life as Toronto manager. His father undoubtedly would have preferred Erroll to follow a more stable business career. Erroll also had an older sister, Mrs. Dorothy Macrae.

In the immediate pre-war years Boyd worked at various jobs including one with the CPR, but the fascination in flying remained with him. During 1912 and 1913 he worked in Saskatoon, Saskatchewan as an automobile salesman where he showed a particular aptitude for mechanics, constructing small models of automobiles and flying machines. A keen sportsman, he was a member of the Saskatoon rugby team and was prominent in all branches of athletics.

He moved to the warmer climate of Bermuda for the winter in 1913 where he dreamed of flying some day. War in Europe, then on the horizon, would provide him with the opportunity to become a pilot – and to lose his youth.

4

Chasing Zeppelins Over England

WORLD WAR I provided the first great adventure for young Erroll Boyd. In Toronto he was commissioned a first lieutenant in the Queens Own Rifles, a regiment in which his father had served. In early 1915 almost everyone thought the war would end soon and local flight training did not yet exist. Not wanting to miss going overseas, Boyd requested leave of absence to proceed to England on his own to try for a commission in the Royal Flying Corps (RFC). Sir Sam Hughes, Minister of Militia, granted permission. The next night the young man boarded a train from Toronto to New York where he caught a steamer to Liverpool, England.

On the ship Erroll shared a cabin with a well-known author, Howard Pritchard Okie, from Washington, D.C. who was then writing a novel, *America and the German Peril*. Okie, about twenty years senior to the young Canadian, was to teach him many things about living and finding his way about the cosmopolitan circles of London.

Upon taking his first physical examination for service in the RFC Boyd was rated colour blind and turned down, but he did not give up. Doubting the test results, he tried the navy. To help his cause, he obtained a letter of recommendation from his relative, Sir George Perley, high commissioner for Canada in England. He passed the slightly different colour test for the Royal Naval Air Service (RNAS). Boyd soon received his commission as probationary flight sub-lieutenant. He was given a few days to get new uniforms before proceeding to the Eastchurch naval air station on the Isle of Sheppey near the mouth of the Thames River.

Flight Sub-Lieut. J.E.D. Boyd, Royal Naval Air Service, 1915 (Courtesy of Boyd Family)

Wishing to celebrate his new status, Erroll and his new friend Okie were in dire need of funds. Okie's mind went to work and developed a plan. Next morning Boyd, still in his Canadian uniform, and Okie, resplendent in morning coat, striped trousers and top hat, proceeded to a banking establishment at 42 Pall Mall where they were ushered into a private office.

After seeing Boyd's papers the banker asked if 200 pounds, then nearly a thousand dollars, would be sufficient. When Erroll told the distinguished official that twenty pounds would be enough, the pleased expression on Okie's face began to wane. However, Boyd's account was credited with the 200, and he immediately drew a draft for twenty after which he and Okie headed for the nearest pub to celebrate. The money had been advanced under the custom that any officer in the Royal Navy was always a good risk.

After living it up in London for a few days, the time arrived for Boyd to report to Eastchurch. Boarding a train at Victoria Station, he first gained full realization that a real war was being fought. He remembered vividly leaving Okie that night, seeing wounded men being taken away on stretchers, and witnessing tearful and possibly last good-byes. The whole atmosphere reeked of war.

Years later Boyd read Okie's novel but noticed an irreverent poem that he had composed in their hotel room in London was missing. It read:

God with us on the soldiers' belts, the Belgian women read,
The soldiers plotted a crown of thorns and put it on his head.
And for each ravished woman, each Belgian child who died,
Again on earth, by Christian hands, our Christ was crucified.
Perhaps the mother's voice too weak, also heaven is too high,
The unanswered Belgian Hagers still see their Ishmaels die!
Just for a strip of North Sea coast and a league of Calais sand
Where the snake may stretch and coil again to strike at other lands!
That is the truth my brother, but this strangest thing,
The children he loved must die – yet God still saves the King.

Dining with Okie years later in the U.S.A. Boyd learned that the poem had been censored from the book as being too sacrilegious for publication.

The following are Boyd's recollections of "British gentlemen" at Eastchurch in 1915:

> After mess, usually, we gambled. The stakes ran high for we were men of means excepting myself, to whom money meant little. What can money mean to men about to die? But always if the next day or the day following, a creditor and a debtor came back from a flight, the debt was paid. The British Navy stood behind all debts contracted by its officers. Gambling debts are debts of honour in England. You may stall off your butcher, your baker, your barber, but you must never avoid paying your bookie or your poker or your bridge debts immediately. To fail to do so is a challenge to suicide, for official social ostracism will trail and haunt you to the end of your official career.

Boyd's flight instructor at Eastchurch was none other than John Alcock, later to be knighted after making the first nonstop transatlantic flight in 1919. Boyd felt Alcock's knowledge of flying ranked him as the best instructor in England.

Each lesson at the Eastchurch Aviation School lasted from seven to ten minutes, and to log an hour required at least half a dozen flights. His first training flight was in a Wright forty-horsepower biplane with a top speed of about fifty mph. Without today's conventional ailerons, it had wing-warping flight controls and two chain-driven propellers.

Under Alcock's expert instruction, Boyd soloed in less than four hours, after accomplishing the art of landings, take-offs and figure eights. Boyd's solo flight was in a Short pusher-type biplane, the same type in which Winston Churchill had flown at Eastchurch. Later Boyd witnessed the death of a fellow Canadian named Alexander in a crash with the same type of plane. In June 1915 Boyd was issued licence No. 1358 issued by the U.K.'s Royal Aero Club, valid anywhere in the British Empire. There is no record of him later having a separate Canadian licence.

The relatively young Winston Churchill as head of the admiralty was primarily responsible for the formation of the separate Royal Naval Air Service in 1912. He took some flight instruction from several instructors but none of them authorized him for solo flight,

Winston Churchill and Short Pusher (Courtesy of Fleet Air Arm Museum)

probably due to his senior government post and possibly due to his wife's wishes. He had commenced such instruction when he was thirty-eight although the normal maximum at the time was thirty-two.

Squadron Leader C. P. O. Bartlett, RNAS, who learned to fly about a year later than Boyd, recalled Eastchurch as a hilarious and very noisy crowd of trainee officers, bawdy songs, and mostly Curtiss aircraft. He recalled John Alcock as the star performer in the following words:

> On coming in to land he would invariably cut his engine at about 2,000 feet, hold up the nose of his aircraft until the propeller stopped, and glide in with such perfect judgment that he always ran on to the tarmac and almost into the hangar with a completely dead engine.

Erroll Boyd wrote to his mother about an early experience in which his chum, Sub-Lieutenant Watson, was killed on June 30, 1915. Newly certified, Boyd and Watson were sent to fly to the commanding officer at Eastbourne, about sixty miles away. Boyd said:

I do not remember how I got out of the storm as Watson fell to the ground 5,000 feet below. We were only a few hundred yards apart and I was really relying on him for my course as he had been flying longer than I. I saw him drop. The air chucked me about like a piece of paper and I cannot realize how I can be here writing to you. Just as soon as I saw Watson drop, I climbed and climbed until I must have reached 11,000 feet. I went above the storm and finally arrived back, but I am a very lucky boy, but am all in over Watson's death.

Another friend, Lieutenant Lester, crashed into the sea in a brand-new machine. The officer was saved but his machine went to the bottom.

Boyd also wrote about a cross-country observation flight on June 20, 1915. He was flying an older Avro biplane with a gravity tank just in front of the pilot. It was filled from a lower tank by a pressure pump. When Boyd adjusted the tap, the fuel flew into his face and he lost control of his aircraft. Near the ground he regained control and landed safely.

Boyd flew many different types of early aircraft in this period.

Short Pusher-type in which Boyd soloed (Courtesy of Fleet Air Arm Museum)

Exchanging letters in 1959 with pioneer pilot Viola Gentry about the OX5 Club (whose members had flown aircraft powered by that engine), he recalled flying one of the first Curtiss JN-4s in England in 1915 and said: "The radiator boiled over and I wonder today how I managed to get down safely."

Boyd served in No. 4 Squadron under Commander Ivor Courtney, one of Winston Churchill's former instructors. In a very short time he became one of the first night-flying pilots in England. Their specific job was to try to shoot down the German Zeppelins which had brought some destruction to London.

"This was easier said than done, especially in the contraptions used in those days," Boyd later wrote. "Night flying was more a matter of getting into the air between biscuit tins filled with salt and petrol used for flares along the field, and arriving safely back at the airport without breaking your neck."

A Zeppelin could hide in the clouds, shut off its motors and drift with the winds. Suspended by cable beneath, a German officer in a small observation car would direct by telephone the course of the flight and the dropping of bombs. By dropping its ballast a Zeppelin could out-climb aircraft of that early stage of the war.

On a summer evening in 1915, Squadron Commander Ivor Courtney received word from intelligence that a German Zeppelin had left its base and was sighted en route heading over the North Sea towards Dover with probable destination of Eastchurch and London. Eastchurch was then the largest naval air station in England. Boyd was ordered to be ready with his ship, a Blackburn B.E.2C powered by a fifty hp Gnome motor. It carried four twenty-pound bombs on its undercarriage. Boyd was to go up as soon as the Zeppelin was sighted, even though his experience was very limited.

The idea was to get above the Zeppelin and drop the bombs on it. The airship would have an observer on top with a machine gun on the alert for enemy machines. There was no machine gun on Boyd's aircraft at this time – only bombs.

The attacking Zeppelin, unaware of its own position but aided by the searchlight seeking it, was soon dropping bombs on the base. Boyd was ordered to take off immediately. Well into the takeoff run, he was suddenly catapulted from his ship. He found himself sitting in a dazed condition in the mud. His ship had run into a crater ripped into the earth by a bomb from the Zeppelin. A short distance away his plane was upside down. Luckily, the four twenty-pound bombs had remained fast to the undercarriage and there was no fire.

Boyd felt he had done his bit of war for the night, but, to his dismay, he heard orders barked that another ship was ready on the line. Taking time only to down a jigger of whiskey which a fellow officer provided, he climbed into a new eighty hp Avro, missed the craters and got aloft.

Under a 1,500-foot cloud ceiling, Boyd followed the Thames towards London, the probable course of the Zeppelin. He saw the flash of anti-aircraft guns streaking upward ahead of him, and the ground searchlights trying to catch the Zeppelin in their glare. When caught in their wavering beams he felt relatively safe as the gunners could see the plane's British markings. In the dark they could only hear his motor, and their ears were not trained to distinguish between the sound of a LeRhone and a German Daimler motor.

Beneath him was the big horseshoe curve of the Thames as it flowed through London. All lights in the city had been turned off. The clouds were breaking, and in the occasional holes he caught a glimpse of the vague shadow of the marauder above. He climbed higher, trying to get above it to drop his bombs. The Zeppelin and Boyd changed course towards Dover on the English Channel. Again the Boche disappeared. Boyd had been flying about an hour and could not get any higher than 4,500 feet. Then he sighted a Zeppelin above and ahead bombing Dover. He later heard that a pier end had been demolished and a destroyer hit.

Boyd chased the almost invisible hulk of the raider out over the sea, but it slid once more into the clouds and was lost. Out over the Dover Straight Boyd realized that his petrol was low. He throttled back, pulled the bomb releases, and dropped the missiles into the sea. Banking sharply, he turned back toward the coast. He decided not to fly cross-country for fear of getting lost, and chose to follow the coastline home. With the fuel low he decided to land short of Eastchurch at Westgate, a field familiar to him in daylight.

Unknown to Boyd, German records obtained after World War II showed that five Zeppelins headed for England if that was the night of August 9-10, 1915, although one turned back near the coast with engine trouble. Commander Wenke, groping through rain clouds in the L10, glimpsed the Thames, and, thinking he was over eastern London, sent down his bombs into what he thought were shipping yards. Twelve of the bombs fell in a line across the landing ground of the Eastchurch naval air station, far down near the mouth of the river. The navigation of the Zeppelins on a cloudy night was frequently very inaccurate. This tends to confirm Boyd's later opinion of commander Courtney's error in turning on the airport's searchlight.

The Zeppelin Boyd chased south of London this night may have been the L12 under commander Peterson. Peterson had climbed from 6,500 to 9,500 feet approaching Dover, which he initially thought was Harwich far to the north. The Dover gunners aimed well and hit cells three and four. The sinking Zeppelin headed southeast for occupied Belgium. At 3:40 a.m. its stern was dragging in the water. A German torpedo boat towed the crippled Zeppelin into Ostend. Three British air pilots from Dunkirk attempted to destroy her, but their bombs missed and one pilot was shot down and killed.

The ineffectiveness of planes of that era against Zeppelins and the dangers of flying them at night were stressed by C.G. Grey, editor of *The Aeroplane*, writing in *The War Illustrated*, on November 6, 1915. He criticized Winston Churchill's promise that any hostile airships would be "met by a swarm of hornets" which would make things remarkably unpleasant for the raiders. He concluded it was not worthwhile chasing airships in the dark with airplanes.

Early in 1916 a special committee report on the British naval air service reported night flying had been ineffective and costly, and recommended better-illuminated, larger aerodromes. It reported that "in eighty-nine sample flights some twenty machines were wholly or partly wrecked, three pilots were killed, and eight pilots were more or less seriously injured."

The first assignment of Billy Bishop, Canada's top ace in the war, was Zeppelin-hunting out of Northholt after gaining his wings in November 1916. He hated this dangerous, unproductive work and found the whole experience akin to being tossed into a lake at midnight.

Boyd said much later that the Zeppelins retained their air supremacy over airplanes for a short period early in the war, but later machines were developed with greater speed, climbing capability and manoeuvrability, providing a balance of power which eventually saw heavier-than-air craft rule the sky.

In spite of its pre-war experience with passenger-carrying airships, Germany had only one Zeppelin for reconnaissance in its navy when war broke out in August 1914. The first crude bombing attack over England did not occur until January 1915. Due to the threat of destruction by anti-aircraft fire, the Zeppelin commanders soon learned to concentrate their attacks at night during the moonless half of the month. Later in the war the hydrogen-filled Zeppelins became much more vulnerable to high-climbing aircraft with incendiary and explosive ammunition.

During the entire war seventeen German airships were lost with all hands, and the fatality rate of their wartime flight crews was about forty per cent. While Erroll Boyd did not catch any Zeppelins in 1915, he at least survived the dangerous night flying missions.

5

Boyd Gets Shot Down

ERROLL BOYD soon would be hunting submarines after his less than successful missions from Eastchurch chasing Zeppelins—but his luck would soon run out. After a short transfer to Dover for further night flying and reconnaissance work, he was sent across the English Channel in September 1915 to a base in Dunkirk near the border between France and Belgium.

Machine guns generally were not mounted on aircraft at this early stage in the hostilities, and pistols and hand grenades were ineffective. Anti-aircraft fire from the ground was a great danger.

A pilot at Dunkirk was usually given orders showing the probable location of friendly British ships in the area just before he climbed into his plane. Boyd's usual run took him northeast off the coast past Nieuport, Ostend and Zeebrugge, then inland to Ghent and southwest over Roulers and Ypres, a distance of about 130 miles. Part of his job was to observe that no submarines were sneaking out of a base in a hidden inlet just north of Zeebrugge and to report on the amount and direction of poison gas being rolled from the German trenches over parts of the battle front.

On one flight Boyd was manoeuvring to take advantage of clouds about eight miles off Ostend when he sighted a grey cigar-like object several miles further out. His orders indicated no British or allied submarine in the area. He throttled back the ninety hp motor of his single-seat Nieuport biplane to glide as quietly as possible towards the sub.

Suddenly one of the white-uniformed sailors spotted him. About a dozen men rushed to go down the hatch as the submarine began to dive. Boyd slowed down his 125 mph dive, levelled off at fifty feet and released his four bombs in rapid succession. With full throttle he banked away to avoid whatever explosion might occur.

Beneath him Boyd stared down at a turmoil of water. He thought he saw oil spread over the surface of the sea. As the Nieuport sped back to Dunkirk, a reaction set in and Boyd's spirits sank. He saw the picture of those men struggling down into the uncertain protection of the submarine's hull. He thought about the fact that he and his enemy were all of the same race and that only man-made barriers and boundaries separated them. Then a different reaction set in as he thought of the submarine crew's mission to torpedo to death thousands in Allied shipping.

His commanding officer sent out several planes to verify his report and to ensure that a school of German subs was not sneaking out of their well-protected base. One of the chaps who flew in that flight never came back and was swallowed up by the sea.

The dispatches of Sir John French, the British Commanding Officer, mentioned this probable submarine sinking, but the Germans much later denied that any subs were sunk by aircraft in 1915. The bombs dropped by the RNAS were relatively small, usually twenty pounds or occasionally sixty-five pounds, but the numerous attacks made on them undoubtedly were a frightening experience for the U-boat crews.

An earlier press report dated August 26 said a squadron commander had sunk and completely wrecked a German submarine which was located along with a German destroyer off the coast near Ostend. The report said it is not the normal practice of the Admiralty to publish statements of such losses where the enemy has no other source of information of the time and place where losses occurred.

The main task of the RNAS at Dunkirk was the bombardment of the coast to avert enemy bombing attacks on the fleet. There were very few encounters with German aircraft along the Belgian coast throughout the year. The enemy relied rather on his increasingly efficient anti-aircraft guns.

On October 3, 1915, Flight Lieutenant Erroll Boyd's luck ran out. Three aircraft took off from Dunkirk before dawn on a forty-mile raid up the coast to Zeebrugge, Belgium, to bomb German hangars and supply sheds. They each carried six sixty-five pound bombs under the fuselage of their machines. Boyd was flying a fast French-built

REP Parasol monoplane and carried an additional dozen or so small hand bombs, weighing five or six pounds each.

They arrived over their targets just as dawn was breaking and dropped their bombs from about two miles up. Shells from the Archies (anti-aircraft guns) began to burst pretty close to them, and the planes got separated. Boyd was pretty close to 11,000 feet and thought these must have been new Archies to reach so high. He climbed until he was a few hundred feet over 12,000 where he felt safe, and began to look around to locate his position. He had passed Zeebrugge so he wheeled around for home base, hungry for a good breakfast.

Suddenly there was a blinding flash in front of him. The propeller and wings were hit and he fell out of control. Fortunately, he was strapped in or he would have beat the aircraft to the ground. After some fancy, unplanned aerobatics, Boyd managed to get the machine under control in time to make a safe forced landing just fifty yards over the Dutch border.

Boyd thought he was in German-controlled territory, and later admitted he must have been "a little balmy in the bean" for offering extensive resistance to his grey-uniformed rescuers, even firing a light pistol at them. The Dutch soldiers finally subdued him and one explained in English that they were not Germans.

As for Boyd's machine, three of the nine cylinders of the LeRhone 110 hp engine were torn away, the propeller was splintered to bits and the wings were badly torn. The plane was later purchased by the Dutch government and refitted with another engine.

During the time Boyd was shot down and interned in October 1915, the great German ace Manfred von Richthofen, who later would shoot down eighty Allied aircraft, was training to be a pilot. The ex-cavalry officer had already served as an observer in a two-seater on both the eastern and western fronts. He would not be credited with his first victory until September 1916, almost a year later. Most of the scores accumulated by aces on both sides occurred towards the latter part of the war when aerial combat greatly intensified.

The great Richthofen, known as the Red Baron, was shot down and killed by a Canadian, Roy Brown, in April 1918, when the German ace was on the tail of another Canadian, the low flying "Wop" May. May later became a renowned bush pilot. Australian machine-gunners on the ground also claimed this victory over the

German ace of aces, and there is some evidence to support their claim.

It is interesting to note that governments on both sides used their great aces as propaganda tools to bolster public support and enthusiasm for the war. While Boyd did not become an ace, his wartime adventures were only beginning.

6

Internment in Holland

AFTER being forced down on October 3, 1915, near Nieuvlist in neutral Dutch territory, Boyd was interned near Bodegraven at the centuries-old Fort Wierickerschans which bore the scars of many European wars. Forty-three other British officers were interned there, after escaping into neutral Holland during the German invasion of Belgium in 1914.

Writing to his mother in Toronto, Lieutenant Boyd wrote:

> It will be news for you to learn that I am safe and have a chance of seeing you again. You will understand of course that I cannot tell you everything in a letter, but hope sometime to be able to relate all my experiences.
>
> I twisted my wrist, and it is a little difficult to write, but I may tell you that I left Dunkirk on Sunday at 5 a.m. to drop bombs on Zeebrugge. I naturally was obliged to go well out to sea and up the coast to escape German observation and anti-aircraft batteries. I did this with a missing engine.
>
> Nearing Zeebrugge I went right into hell and when I came into the line of their shells, they hit my machine five times; if I had had a passenger, he would have been killed. When my engine was hit I was 12,000 feet in the air which, thank God, enabled me to glide into Holland under the most awful fire from the German batteries and land in a beet field. However, I dropped my bombs, and here I am, safe and sound.

It looks as if I must stay locked up here at the fort till the end of the war. If Holland comes in, however, I will have a chance to see some more fighting. Everybody here thinks I should be happy and not worrying, as I had a most miraculous escape from death.

While the long, desolate hours in internment were mostly spent gambling, the moisture of the fort and Holland in general won Boyd over to an old Dutch custom: to chase the dampness from his bones he acquired a taste for gin.

The nearly 1,500 men of the Royal Naval Brigade, on the other hand, were interned at nearby Groningen. While kept under discipline, they enjoyed a large amount of liberty making a community in itself with a vigorous social life with many organized activities. "If I had the choice," Boyd wrote, "I would vastly prefer to be a private at Groningen than one of the officers at Wierickerschans."

In December 1915, Boyd and the other officers were paroled to any unfortified part of Holland, with the promise of the British government that they would not escape. Boyd chose to live in The Hague with considerable freedom to come and go as he pleased, as long as he stayed within prescribed limits. He said Holland was full of German secret service men.

REP Parasol-type in which Boyd was shot down (Courtesy of Fleet Air Arm Museum)

Life in The Hague was much more pleasant than at the old fort. The palace of Queen Wilhelmina was open house to all British officers who cared to drop in for tea. On many occasions they talked with the gracious queen and on one occasion Boyd had the pleasure of ice skating with Princess Juliana who later became queen.

Boyd became friendly with Count Falk, son of the minister to the queen. He also met and dated a beautiful Polish girl who later caused him concern. He was informed by his superior officer, Admiral Purefoy, that the charming young lady was a German spy and was about to be deported to her home. He later learned that upon her return she was taken into custody and accused by the Germans of being a British spy, and was sent to a prison camp for the duration of the war.

One night in February 1916, Boyd was in the American Grill in The Hague when he met Joseph J. O'Neill. Hearing a little English spoken in a Dutch setting, Boyd said to him: "You're an American, aren't you? My name's Boyd. I am a Canadian by birth but I've spent so much time in the States that I'm almost a Yank . . . Sit down."

Boyd didn't begin to talk airplanes. Instead, he asked what shows were running in New York, how 42nd Street and Broadway looked, and what new steps were being used in the dances. When he later heard that O'Neill was from the New York newspaper, *The World*, he remarked:

> I know a chap who was going to do a stunt for your paper. Remember Porte – Lieut. John Cyril Porte – who was going to fly across the ocean in the America (built by Glenn Curtiss) just before the war broke out? I met him at Hendon where he was giving flying lessons last year. Fine chap, Porte, but I don't think he'd ever have got over the water in the old America. She didn't have power enough to get up high and she was altogether too slow. They had her in the Channel last year, scouting, but she wasn't much good.

Two weeks later *The World* came out with a feature story occupying almost a full page with the following captions:

"BOYDIE" ESCAPES A GERMAN PRISON BY
ONLY 50 YARDS

But the Daring Canadian Flight Lieutenant "Strafes His Luck" None the Less Because He was Shot Down on Dutch Territory, and Internment There Keeps Him Out of the Game That He Dearly Loves.

HIS OWN THRILLING STORY OF HIS ILL-FATED TRIP

He Had Dropped Six 75-Pound Bombs Upon German Hangars at Zeebrugge and Was Headed for Home When an Archie Smashed His Propeller – Mistook Dutchmen for Germans When He Landed

The long story concluded that it was the ambition of the stocky Canadian chap to do what Lieutenant John Cyril Porte was going to do for *The World* – fly across the Atlantic Ocean. "As sure as we're sitting here, I'll do it some time, too," Boyd said.

> But I won't do it as Porte was going to – that is, by a jump from Newfoundland to the Azores, then to Spain and then to England. I'm for making one bite of it – starting off in a bus that can make 150 miles an hour and sticking right to it until I get over. I've been up for nine hours, though of course I didn't maintain any such speed. It's 1,900 miles   across, and I think it could be made in fifteen hours at the outside, with favourable winds. (Alcock and Brown made it in 16 hours and 27 minutes in June 1919.)
>
> The first thing I'm going to do when the war is over is fly from Bermuda to the United States. I have spent some time in Bermuda. The trip across to the States is one that's never been made yet. I think it will be easy. It's 800 miles, and with a good bus it ought to be made in well under eight hours. The United States is a good big mark to hit, so I'd be sure not to miss it. Wouldn't that stunt make a good article for The World! I'll take you along if you'll come.

Journalist O'Neill declined the invitation saying it was too futuristic to make a positive commitment.

In May of 1916 Boyd was allowed six months leave of absence to return to North America, reporting periodically to the Dutch legation. He sailed from Rotterdam to New York on the *S.S. Noordam*, following which he spent much time in New York and Toronto. In August a Toronto doctor examined Boyd and concluded he was in an extremely nervous condition and that his return to the atmosphere of war in Holland would prejudice his recovery. An added factor, the doctor wrote, would be the poor state of health of his mother.

When the six months were up, Boyd embarked on the *S.S. Adriatic* for Holland. Before passing the Ambrose Light Ship, he received a wireless message extending his leave for two months. It arrived in time for him to leave with the pilot boat.

In December 1916 he was compelled to return to The Hague, sailing again on the *Adriatic* from New York on the day before Christmas. The ship, laden with munitions, tanks, Seldon trucks and only three passengers, arrived in Liverpool eleven days later. Boyd then sailed from Gravesend, England, for Holland on the *Prince Hendrick*, a small side-wheeler loaded with mail and thousands of empty barrels to hold the ship afloat in case of striking a mine. Ordinarily a six-hour trip, it took fifteen hours due to stormy weather. At times the crew saw chains of mines bobbing up in the sea. The adventuresome Boyd, the only passenger on board, spent the entire voyage on the bridge with the Dutch captain. The captain had lost his ship on his previous voyage but fortunately the crew had been saved by a British trawler. Boyd later learned that the *Prince Hendrick* was captured by the Germans on its next trip and taken into Zeebrugge.

Four and a half months later Boyd was again paroled from Holland, arriving in New York City in the early summer of 1917. He would not return again to Holland until flying there after his transatlantic flight. This second leave was arranged by Admiral Purefoy from the British legation in The Hague and approved by a Dutch board of doctors.

In March 1917, Erroll Boyd was promoted to full Lieutenant in the RNAS. When the latter service was merged with the Royal Flying Corps in April 1918, Boyd was gazetted as a captain in the Royal Air Force. In the civilian life ahead of him he would captain many aircraft.

7

Letters Home About War

ERROLL BOYD'S dramatic experiences in the air were described to his older brother Norman in letters written during Erroll's internment in the Dutch castle at Wierickerschans. Carrying no date, the letters were probably written in late 1915.

I was shot down by the German anti-aircraft batteries at Zeebrugge on Sunday, October 3rd, and managed to make Dutch territory with my aeroplane in a crippled condition. Being interned at the above place with considerable time on my hands I will endeavor to give you some idea of what we are doing in the line of flying at the front and in England.

As Flight Sub-Lieutenant Homer Smith has already stated in a published letter that we have them licked to a frazzle, this would appear to be quite true, as they generally do turn tail as soon as they see one of our machines. We have a patrol from Dunkirk daily weather permitting, and we fly to Brussels and Ghent, etc., some seventy miles over the lines, but it is very seldom you see a German machine venture over our lines, in fact I only saw three in all the time I was at the front.

You certainly have to hand it to the Flying Corps for their wonderful work, not only for the bomb dropping raids, but for reconnaissance they perform daily, especially the Royal Flying Corps, which have mostly dual machines. These fellows carry out some of the most exciting and dangerous flights, and the Royal Navy Service are proud to take their hats off to them.

The French airmen fly mostly Voisins, a French pusher machine. I have seen them leave the aerodrome at Dunkirk say at ten o'clock p.m. loaded up with bombs, go over the lines, come back and perhaps do this three to four times in one night. I remember quite well two Frenchmen who used to go duck shooting in their machine, which of course is a pusher type. They would fly about ten feet above the swamp just behind the aerodrome, stand up in their machines and shoot the ducks. I can tell you it was a treat to see them. We all used to turn out for this little performance which took place occasionally.

Air raids occur almost daily. We are generally told the evening before, or perhaps two hours before we are to leave, just what our objective is going to be, leaving in the dark and arriving at daylight over the spot which we intend to bomb. It is great sport and very exciting. As many as twenty aeroplanes go together at times, and you can imagine the hail of bombs a town would get if every machine carried six bombs, which is the usual number, although some carry a less number of heavier weight. Very often you see our aeroplanes come back simply riddled with bullet holes and the pilot smiling as if nothing had happened.

Before I left for the front flying at night was an ordinary course with me. Some wayside farmer imagines he hears a Zep, and he at once informs the authorities and perhaps after all what he heard was a motor cycle on the road. Of course in many other cases it really is a Zep, but we generally get good information beforehand. Flying at night is no joke, and a good many accidents occur this way; I should think fifteen per cent at the least.

In the case of Flight Sub-Lieutenant Hilliard, who was killed at Yarmouth a short time ago, he went up after a Zep, and not having any luck he returned to the aerodrome, and while landing in the dark his under carriage was swept off and the six bombs he was carrying exploded and blew him and his machine to Kingdom Come. Then in the case of Flight Sub-Lieutenant Lord, one of our squadron, he went up at Westgate, and on landing his machine turned over and he was crushed to death beneath it. Flying at night is all right when you are in the air, but then there is the landing, and if you have an engine failure, your only chance is to make for the sea, and, as you know, the water is pretty cold this time of the year. One consolation is you can always see the water.

I have no doubt that the great progress in aviation will cause machines to be made which will catch these Zeppelin Huns, and I am sincerely looking forward to that time. I should not wonder if the next Zeps to appear over London will have a hot time of it, as they are really getting busy now erecting very powerful aircraft guns on the buildings, etc.

It is a wonderful sight to be over the City of London at night with all the search lights going full pelt on a Zep, and you can see the anti aircraft guns at work. One must do this to realize the tense excitement. You can easily see the Thames and the long line of bridges when these immense search lights are turning. One forgets all about getting home, landing and engine troubles. These things do not come into heads at all; what you want to do is find the Zep and bring him down. I believe a great many of the boys would rush into a Zep rather than let it get away if they could.

I remember one Zeppelin which was brought down by the late Flight Sub-Lieutenant Warneford, V.C. in the daylight, and the last one which came down off Ostend in the dusk of the morning by anti aircraft. Flight Lieutenant Keith Johnson was shot down after taking part in this, and I think they found his body off Ostend in the water. His brother was killed taking his ticket. He had a collision with Flight Lieutenant Alexander, a Canadian, who was also killed, his machine catching fire so that he was burned to death. It seems tough on the Johnson parents, having two sons killed in the air service inside of a month.

The Royal Naval Air Service has some wonderful

machines, the double engine Caudron, 250 hp in all, doing a speed of 100 miles an hour and climbing at the rate of 5,000 feet in seven minutes, with passenger, two bombs and a machine gun. This is the kind Lieut. Homer Smith flew for a while at the front. Then there are monoplanes, Moranes by name, which are wonderful. Warneford's machine was a Morane. Then the REP with 110 hp Le Rhone engines doing a speed of 100 miles an hour and climbing at the rate of 1,000 feet per minute. The Nieuport biplane is our best fighting engine, carrying two Lewis guns, the pilot in front and the passenger having a range over the top plane and also over the cab. These engines are very fast, and will stand any kind of weather.

Flight Sub-Lieutenant Mulock, a Canadian from Winnipeg, blew up the sheds in Brussels while in one of these machines. Some pilot, Mulock. He had to fly back in the rain, and a regular southwest gale blowing. Then the latest type, a Morane biplane, with 110 hp Le Rhone, will climb 7,000 feet in six minutes. This is hard to believe, but nevertheless true, and it has a speed of 125 miles an hour, we are told. We certainly are making great progress, and I feel rather a nut being locked up here and not able to help out. However, I suppose I must bear with my misfortune with the best grace possible.

On my first trip to the front I was told to go up and take a look at the front, and after lunch I got C.P.O. Gott to come along with me. He brought an old rifle in case of an attack and ten rounds of ammunition, my machine not being equipped with a machine gun. Mulock had told me never to turn tail if I happened to run into any German Taubes, but to go right over the lines and take a good look while I was at it. We started off at about 2:30 p.m., climbed to 11,000 feet and made for the front. I can tell you it was great, although I had some experience reaching the firing line. I thought I would just go a mile or two over. Well, if we didn't run right into two German Taubes. They came straight at us, and I sure got the cold shivers up my back. However, Gott loaded his rifle and I will never forget the look on his face. I went straight for them, and they did likewise with us, while you could see their machine gun going full pelt at us, and we were helpless in a way, but I was determined not to run because they would be sure to get me if I did, so we kept straight on them till I should judge we were within 500 or 600 yards, and sure enough they turned and made for home double time, I doing likewise, and when we were passing the lines on our way home, they gave us a terrible fire with their anti aircraft guns. It was my first trip over the lines, and to see those big black puffs of smoke coming made me a bit nervous. However, I managed to get home without injury. C.P.O. Gott sure had an exciting tale to tell his fellow mechanics. It was a great experience giving me a good idea what I was to go through in raids later on, but I got used to all this in time.

It is wonderful how few casualties there are in the air considering the very hazardous work that takes place daily. Wind and clouds make no difference to flying in the war; in fact, when we raid any position, we generally pick out a cloudy day.

Homer Smith's Exploits

Homer Smith, Boyd's friend from his early days in the Queen's Own Regiment, was one of the first two aviators to complete their tests for pilot certificates at the Curtiss Long Branch aviation course in Toronto in the summer of 1915.

To qualify for his certificate, Smith was required to fly two flights alone without an instructor on board. The tests consisted of many figure eights flown around two poles and a spot landing with the engine shut off above 300 feet. J.A.D. McCurdy, Canada's first pilot, telegraphed that Smith was leaving immediately for service overseas with the RNAS.

Later that same year Homer Smith wrote to his mother:

I was stationed at Margate when four of us received a telegram to fly to Eastchurch. Once there we were told to leave for Dunkirk the next morning, and I was to fly a huge machine with two ten-cylinder engines, two propellers and three bodies. It is the most wonderful thing I have ever flown. I left at 7 a.m. and arrived Dunkirk at 7:45 a.m.

Believe me the Germans are indeed wonderful, but as far as the air is concerned, we have them licked to a frazzle. They never fly across our lines, but in spite of their wonderful anti-aircraft guns, we fly as much as sixty miles into their country, actually running a regular patrol that far twice a day. Two days ago I flew thirty miles into their territory with four others on other machines, and for my huge double engine machine I had a passenger, a machine gun, two sixty-five-pound high explosive bombs and four twenty-pound bombs.

I dropped the bombs and returned down the coast. It was very exciting indeed. We never "cross the line" under 10,000 feet, and I crossed at 12,000. They got my range though, and in spite of my circling and diving, they put two holes in the seat of the aircraft and four in the wings. It is great. They fire huge shells which burst and make terrible puffs of black smoke. I flew in over Ypres and out over Nieuport. At Ypres they fire shrapnel and Nieuport, high explosives, but do not be afraid because we have lost no pilots as yet. Yesterday "Red" Mulock from Winnipeg flew away in to Brussels, descended to a few hundred feet, and blew up the Zeppelin sheds there with the Zeppelins in them. The commanding officer gave him a toast in the mess, and I think he will get either the V.C. or D.S.O. He had to fly seventy miles back in pitch darkness, frightful rain and a blizzard.

It was great. We only have to fly about once a week. It is a cinch and we have the best mess I have ever seen. It is run by one of our men who was the Duke of Westminster's butler. Tell Mrs. Boyd that Erroll is happy and well and that we fly together as often as possible.

Smith's letter concluded by saying that he thought he was only there temporarily and would return to Eastchurch "when I will have my Daimler again. She is a peach indeed."

8

A Romantic Wartime Marriage

IN AUGUST of 1914 Canada entered the Great War, and, like other men of that day, young Boyd was eager to join the military. He entered officers' training school in Toronto, and was commissioned a first lieutenant in the Queens Own Rifles, the regiment in which his father had served many years before.

In September of that year he met the woman who would later become his wife: the beautiful nineteen-year-old Evelyn Carbery, a dental surgeon's daughter. She was playing at Toronto's Alexander Theatre in the hit show, *Whirl of the World*, an outstanding musical comedy which had just completed a long run at the Winter Garden Theatre in New York City. It had been Sigmund Romburg's Broadway debut. Willie and Eugene Howard headed the long list of stars in the show, which also included Lucille Cavanaugh, who later gained fame with her dancing act in the Ziegfield Follies. The parents of Jackie Coogan were also with the troupe. Boyd later learned after his marriage that Evelyn used to babysit occasionally with "The Kid" when Jackie was about a year old.

Erroll was introduced to Evelyn by Homer Smith, an officer's training instructor at the Toronto Armoury. Boyd recalled that one evening after Evie's performance they went for a ride on the outskirts of Toronto in the Boyd family car, one of the few National Four sports cars in Canada.

Automobiles were not very common in 1914, and Evie felt the challenge to drive so Erroll let her. She had difficulty keeping a straight line, and Homer commented from the back seat: "What the hell are you trying to do, Evie – write your name all over the road?"

Evelyn Carbery's show played a full week in Toronto without Erroll missing a single performance. Her short stay was unforgettable, but the show left for Buffalo and Erroll was not to meet her again until the spring of 1917 following his internment in neutral Holland.

During his second parole Boyd met Evie again in New York. She was then a member of the cast of the play *Cousin Lucy*, starring Julian Eltings. Accompanying her at this reunion was her sister, Ruth, who later became a Max Sennett bathing beauty and graced the first cover of *Life* magazine. Evie and Erroll had maintained correspondence since their first meeting in Toronto in 1914.

They met often. On a rainy July 11th night they were at the well known Churchill's night spot and restaurant as guests of Captain Churchill and Eddie Foy, Sr. As they lingered and watched night break into day, they made up their minds to get married immediately. They rode around the city in a taxicab for a few hours until the shops opened. They purchased a wedding band, obtained a licence and were married at the city hall.

Erroll and Evie had planned to fly to Atlantic City but the weather intervened so they returned to Boyd's apartment at 137th St. and Riverside Drive. There they found Boyd's friend, Reginald Bertram, a survivor of the famous Princess Pat regiment, who was forgetting his wartime experiences with the aid of a bottle of scotch.

It was not long before the newspapers in New York and Toronto were carrying stories with such captions as "Musical comedy star marries world war aviator."

Erroll's mother was soon calling from Toronto. Her first words were "Who is she?"

"My wife, mother dear," Erroll answered.

Great excitement prevailed in the Boyd household in Toronto over this rather unexpected and unpredicted marriage. Erroll's mother, father, sister Dorothy and her dog took off in the family car for the long trip to New York to meet the new family member. Three days later Evelyn and Erroll travelled to Albany to meet them. Erroll remembered well the surprised expression on their faces when they first saw the gorgeous young musical comedy star their son had shanghaied into marriage.

Erroll took the wheel of the new forty hp Page and all his passengers "wrapped their dusters about them." He wheeled down the dusty dirt and macadam roads to New York. They sped along at speeds up to fifty-five mph along the thirty-five mph top-limit roads of the day.

During their stay in New York the family wined and dined at such famous night spots as the Peek Inn, Moulin Rouge, Rectors, Shanleys, Ziegfield Roof and Risenwebbers.

"As I was still on service pay, dad was footing much of the money for these excursions," Boyd said. "He was beginning to feel the burden of the expense, so it was decided we would pack and honeymoon back in Toronto. The return trip was made with little trouble with the exception of a boiling radiator and a broken axle that detained us three days in Geneva, N.Y. The trip provided much time for my new wife and my mother to get acquainted."

Back in New York after their Toronto honeymoon, the newlyweds were kept very busy. Evelyn had many friends in show business, including Al Jolson with whom she played in two Winter Garden Shows. Jolson would later appear in the first important talking motion picture, the 1927 Warner Brothers film *The Jazz Singer*. The famed *Mammy* singer threw a great party for them. As Boyd said, "These were days of fast, reckless living which saw the soldier set on a pedestal."

"The age of hero worshipping had a good foothold in the U.S. by then and many were the times the air force uniform I was wearing received undivided attention," he later said. "Everyone wanted to do something for the boys and most fortunately one of their first acts was to pick up a check."

Erroll Boyd's parents in Toronto were well connected to many prominent citizens of the era, some of whom Erroll later described as "social parasites" who had been critical of him for "marrying that theatrical woman." Erroll recalled a function in Toronto on Armistice Day, Nov. 11, 1918, when Lady Beck said: "Erroll Boyd, if you don't bring that beautiful wife of yours out to see us, we are going to disown you."

"Lady Beck, don't you think it is a little late?" he replied.

During his wartime period in New York, Boyd made numerous trips to Buffalo to test the Curtiss JN-4s with OX motors. His fellow tests pilots at the Niagara Street airport were Victor Carlstrom, Phil Rader and Peter Campbell. All three were eventually killed in crashes.

Boyd's own experience in testing resulted in one serious crackup on July 1, 1917, from which he managed to walk away. It occurred at

Mitchell Field, Mineola, Long Island. Boyd was testing the *Lanzius I*, the first all-metal welded plane which incorporated a changeable angle of incidence. Its designer, George Lanzius, was an inventor originally from Holland.

Under the caption, "Lucky Toronto Aviator," the *Montreal Gazette* carried the following story from New York:

> Flt. Lt. Erroll Boyd, RNAS, plunged 300 feet at the Mineola, Long Island field Saturday evening while testing an untried biplane of unique design. His seat belt broke and he was thrown clear of the crash. When rescuers arrived, he was standing near the wreckage puffing on a cigarette. The accident was caused by a defective aileron. In a bombing raid on Zeebrugge he was shot down near the Dutch border. Reaching Holland he was interned, but was allowed to go to America on parole, arriving May 30. He is a 25 year old Toronto native and "a daring driver of racing automobiles."

The Lanzius Aircraft Company had the manufacturing facilities of three factories in New York, Tennessee and New Jersey, and executive offices on Broadway according to their advertisement.

Their variable-speed plane of cantilever construction embodied new aviation principles. The first pilot to take it up, Boyd felt its principles were good, including a quick take-off, fast speed in the air, slow landing and good load capacity. He forecast that the cantilever construction would be adopted by all airplane manufacturers.

Boyd lost control during its test flight and crashed. He later learned that its first Duesenburg engine was thrust through the panel board and was sitting in the seat he had occupied moments before. Boyd did not realize that he had been hurt and went to a dance that night. Three days later it was determined that he suffered a minor concussion and remembered little during the interval after the crash.

Forty years later a former reporter of *Aerial Age* wrote to Boyd his recollections as a witness to this accident:

> I believe you were in a Canadian uniform. As you took off in the plane it began to bank to the right. We saw the ailerons move to correct this, but the plane was so

unstable that the bank increased and the plane smacked in on one wing, nose down. When it hit you were catapulted out of the cockpit and landed some 30 feet away, shaken but unhurt. Lanzius, who witnessed all this, was furious at the damage to his plane, and completely ignored your miraculous escape from injury or worse.

In 1918 George Lanzius built four scouting aircraft for the army air service fitted with the powerful 400 hp Liberty engine. Little further was heard about him or his firm when company pilot L.E. Holt was killed when the Lanzius aircraft he was flying shed its wings.

Between his RNAS pay and the test piloting, Boyd was doing reasonably well financially, but was probably a liberal spender. He did a little writing and numbered among his friends Joseph Jefferson O'Neill who had penned a story in the *New York World* the year previously about Boyd's ambitions to someday fly to Bermuda and across the Atlantic Ocean. It took many years, but Boyd would later realize these ambitions.

The air along the streets of New York in those days was filled with the strains of Gitz Rice's famous song, *Dear Old Pal of Mine*. Boyd's association with Rice brought out the naval officer's talent for writing songs and music. In 1917 Boyd's first song, *For Love of Liberty*, was published by Theodore Metz, writer of *A Hot Time in the Old Town Tonight*. Boyd's patriotic number was fast gaining popularity but dropped out of earshot when the Armistice was signed.

In 1918 Boyd was listed as president of the Manhattan Aircraft Company of New York City, but no record is available of this venture. Erroll had survived the first world war, entered a life-long, happy and productive marriage that would produce five girls, and gained experience as a test pilot.

9

Enter the Roaring Twenties

THE DECADE after the war to end all wars was an exciting time, but one which offered little opportunity for steady employment in aviation in North America. While over ninety-five per cent of the returning airmen sought regular jobs, some became barnstormers flying from town to town offering members of the public their first aerial ride. One of these barnstormers, when asked the greatest risk in this type of work, replied without hesitation, "It's the risk of starving to death."

Even the great feat of Alcock and Brown in flying the Atlantic Ocean nonstop in 1919 did not attract widespread public interest or investment in this new mode of transport. Conditions did not change much until after Charles Lindbergh's nonstop solo flight from New York to Paris in 1927.

Ripley's *Believe It or Not* column became famous when he wrote that seventy persons had flown the Atlantic before Lindbergh. After receiving thousands of protest letters from an unbelieving public, Ripley described them in a subsequent column which included information about the airship flights in 1919 and 1924.

Erroll Boyd later recalled that, in the immediate post-war period, $10,000 war planes were selling for as little as $500 with few takers. He recalled that Frithioff Ericson, who claimed to be a descendant of the famed explorer Leif Ericson, was selling surplus planes which he displayed in the lobby of Toronto's King Edward Hotel.

Unable to land a job in aviation, Boyd was occupied with managing the York Garage on Bloor Street in Toronto where he operated a car rental business with a fleet of fifteen Fords for public hire at one dollar an hour. After publishing his patriotic war song in 1917, he continued his interest in this field, and hit the jackpot with a number called *Dreams*. This initiated a return to New York where he took an office in the Astor Theater building on the west side of Broadway at 45th Street.

Tragedy struck the Boyd family during this stay. Boyd's three-year-old daughter, Jean, was killed in a six-storey fall from their apartment. She was playing a recording of *Dreams* on the phonograph as she sat by the window. A flower box on which she was leaning gave way as she was picking a bouquet of geraniums for her mother. She lost her balance and tumbled to her death – one of the bleakest moments in the Boyd family.

One news report, captioned "Daughter of song writer falls six stories to death," questioned how a song can be written when the soul of the singer is numb with grief. Erroll had passed the shadow of death so many times in his flying career only to have it claim his little Jean.

Evelyn Boyd's health was jeopardized at this time as she was carrying their fourth child, but the Boyds took the little girl's body to Toronto for burial. The ceremony was officiated by Canon Cody, rector of St. Paul's Anglican Church on Bloor Street. The words Cody spoke that day helped both parents to reach some understanding as to why such tragedies happen. After the funeral they returned to New York.

Boyd decided to quit writing songs and went into the hotel management business. Around this same time Bill Shanley of restaurant renown and Erroll were together in the Tijuana Club when the famous fighter, Bill Brennan, was shot and killed by two gunmen in the club lobby. These were the days of prohibition, speakeasies and gang rule.

Brennan, who gave Jack Dempsey one of the toughest fights of his career, had just told Boyd and Shanley that two swarthy characters wanted to collect on a load of liquor from Montreal that had been hijacked. Brennan thought they were trying to collect two payments for one load. He was called to the lobby and Boyd and Shanley heard deafening gun shots. They made a quick exit and the assailants apparently escaped through another exit. Such was life in New York in the roaring twenties.

In those days of bootleg booze and little cellar joints, nearly everyone supplemented their beverage diet with a small still in the kitchen. The first time Boyd tried brewing beer, he used the bathtub for fermentation of the black hops which kept everyone from taking a bath for about four days until the brew was ready for bottling. He then capped about twenty quarts, wiring down the corks to hold the pressure within in event of additional fermentation. Erroll stored the bottles in his wife's wardrobe closet.

Early one morning he was awakened by a sound like pistol shots. The family investigated and found broken glass, a wet floor and the pungent odour of beer throughout the closet. Nearly all his wife's clothes were ruined in the experiment!

For a while in 1924 Boyd had tried his hand at skywriting. Although he had quit writing songs after his daughter's tragic death, he still had six on the market. He attempted to write the title of the songs in the sky for a unique bit of advertising. This venture ended with some minor plane damage while taking off at Long Beach, Long Island.

Erroll returned to the hotel business where he had many friends. He became manager of the Lennox Hotel on 44th Street, a spot patronized by movie stars including two famous Canadians, Mary Pickford, known as "America's sweetheart," and Marie Dressler, a character actress. Boyd later worked in a management capacity at the Rutledge Hotel and at the Stratford House.

During this time the versatile Boyd did several stunts for Pathe News. In his teens he had made many records in Canada racing and paddling canoes. Tricks in canoeing were right up his alley. His first stunt was a drop from a thirty-foot bridge across the Harlem River, while standing in the canoe! He received $500 for this stunt, a good sum of money in those days. He was hired by fight promoter Tex Rickard to perform canoeing stunts in the pool when the Luxor Baths opened on West 47th Street.

In 1926 Boyd joined the British firm of Crosse and Blackwell of marmalade fame as head of its Michigan office in Detroit. While there he owned a Waco biplane and flew it from a small field on the outskirts of the city. Then the great day came when Lindbergh made his nonstop hop to Paris – a catalyst for aviation progress. It gave Erroll the impetus to return to aviation as a means of livelihood.

Boyd approached Crosse and Blackwell's manager in New York and asked for company backing in the building of a plane capable of a nonstop solo flight from New York to Moscow. Eddie Stinson had designed such a plane and Boyd felt competent to fly it. Schlee and

Brock made a spectacular flight in 1927 from Detroit eastbound to Tokyo in eighteen days with stops at several cities in one of Stinson's aircraft. Boyd had done some test flying for Stinson Aircraft at Northville, Michigan.

Crosse and Blackwell, however, did not accept Boyd's proposal. The Stinson aircraft he had hoped to acquire was purchased by a group of businessmen in Brunswick, Georgia, to finance Paul Redfern on a long distance flight. Redfern took off from Brunswick, Georgia, on August 25, 1927, and headed into South America on a flight which ended in oblivion somewhere in the jungle.

Three years later, many independent reports came out of South America of a white man alive in the jungle depths. Much later jungle bush pilot Jimmy Angel reported flying over Redfern's plane many times as it settled deeper into the Venezuelan jungle canopy – but the mystery of Redfern's fate remains unsolved.

Without the cooperation of his employer Crosse and Blackwell, Boyd's future in aviation appeared uncertain. He found a job, however, as a pilot for John Dodge of automobile renown, and resigned from the British firm. He was recommended for the new job by Dodge's former pilot, Johnny Towns of Hamilton, Ontario, who went with Stinson to prepare for a transcontinental air race. Boyd also acquired a Stinson FB-1 biplane with a Wright J-4 engine, and did considerable barnstorming throughout Michigan.

Erroll's daughter, Honor Boyd Smith, recalled many years later that her mother enjoyed greatly the stability of their family life in Detroit when her husband was often home.

Erroll Boyd left Detroit either in the late summer or autumn of 1927. For a short time he took a position with Canadian Transcontinental Airways flying the mail between Montreal and Rimouski where it was transferred to ships operating to and from Liverpool, England.

Boyd was a close friend of the colourful C.A. "Duke" Schiller, who, along with Romeo Vachon, were the two senior pilots of this company operating mainly in the St. Lawrence River valley. Both pilots were later involved in the heroic rescue of the *Bremen* fliers who made the first east-to-west nonstop Atlantic crossing from Ireland to Greenly Island off the northern tip of Newfoundland. The fascinating story of this thirty-six hour flight is described in detail in Fred Hotson's book, *The Bremen*.

Before the winter freeze-up, Boyd accepted an offer in Mexico from George Rihl, later to become a senior vice-president with Pan-American World Airways. Boyd's short assignment in Canada had rekindled his dream to become the first Canadian to fly the Atlantic Ocean. Before the roaring twenties ended, his new experience in Mexico would provide him with the instrument capability to realize that ambition.

10

Down Mexico Way

IN MEXICO Captain Erroll Boyd would gain the instrument flying skills to enable him two years later to make the very first flight across the North Atlantic Ocean outside the summer season. In early 1928 he left Canada to meet Mexicana's chief pilot, Ed Snyder, in Chicago to ferry a Fairchild 41 to Tampico, Mexico. On the flight down they stopped off at Brownsville, Texas, where Boyd met his new employer, George Rihl. Rihl later became senior vice-president with a new company, Pan American, that had operated its first scheduled flight only on October 28, 1927, on the Key West-Havana route.

In Brownsville Erroll had his initiation to the potent Mexican drink, tequila. Major Law, an old-time pilot who operated three planes flying fish from Mexico to Brownsville, was also the tequila courier. The following morning Snyder and Boyd left for Tampico, Boyd's base for the next few months, on a route over which he would often fly later, becoming a pioneer in the carriage of Mexico-U.S.A. airmail.

George Rihl, a U.S. citizen, was active during the early 1920s in oil-well drilling in Mexico. He had joined pilot William "Slim" Mallory in 1924 to organize the flying of payrolls to inaccessible mining camps in the Tampico area as surface travel was unsafe due to banditry. The sacks of currency were dropped from the air.

Rihl, who was an experienced businessman, had organized Compania Mexicana de Aviacion, S.A., (CMA), known as Mexicana. By 1926 the company had a mail contract on the hazardous route between Mexico City and Tampico via Tuxpan, and later flew to Matamoros near the U.S. frontier. Sherman Fairchild, renowned as a leader in aerial photography, acquired a twenty per cent interest in CMA or Mexicana. He introduced the efficient Fairchild aircraft to the company in 1927, used on the first passenger service between Mexico City and the U.S.

Boosting aviation at this time was the flying visit of Charles Lindbergh to Mexico City in late 1927 and early 1928. It was on this visit that Lindbergh met Anne Morrow, daughter of the U.S. ambassador, who would later become his wife. Lindbergh had joined the new Pan American company (later Pan American World Airways) as technical adviser and was making a preliminary exploratory circuit of Central America and the Caribbean for young Juan Trippe, about to initiate his airline's dynamic expansion.

In early 1929 Pan American acquired the entire stock of Mexicana (CMA), which benefitted George Rihl who joined Pan Am's executive ranks. Even before this happened, the year 1928 was one of great achievement for Mexicana. Passengers were carried on the Mexico City-Tampico route. Boyd was also involved in the longer extension to Merida in the Yucatan Peninsula which was opened in October 1928, a route formerly involving very lengthy land and sea journeys.

Erroll Boyd played a pioneering role in many early Mexican endeavors, first flying Hisso Standards over the mountain areas dropping payrolls in leather sacks for the oil companies working in remote regions. One of the sacks of heavy silver pesos accidentally went clear through the roof of a building, fortunately unoccupied at the time.

Flying passengers and mail in Mexico in 1928 was quite primitive. There were no radios and no emergency landing fields. The planes were generally overloaded and their runs were often over uncharted jungles. The chief pilot customarily took a newcomer over the route at least once. Erroll Boyd wrote one early experience:

> The late Eddie Snyder in 1928 took me on my first run over the Mexico City route, and provided a breathtaking experience of blind flying. At 6:00 a.m. we left the Tampico airport with a large quantity of mail and three passengers.
>
> I was most surprised at the heavy load since I had been flying these same ships, Fairchild 71s, where the

Canadian government authorized payload was 400 pounds under that of the Mexican limits.

Eddie got the ship off alright taking practically the entire field. We were supposed to stop at Tuxpan about 100 miles east of Tampico along the coast, but in order to save a few miles, we flew about 10 miles inland. However, we never saw Tuxpan as this town was engulfed in fog.

Passing up this point, Eddie turned the ship southward for the long, steady pull up and over the mountains, and when I say mountains, that is just what I mean! Tuxpan to Mexico City is about 160 miles, and in bad weather you are compelled to climb up through the clouds to an altitude of 12,000 feet, making sure that you will clear the mountain peaks.

Never in the history of my flying career had I become more enthused over the ability of a pilot. Snyder literally put the ship into the clouds, setting his stabilizer for a slow climb. He did not touch the stick, just used his rudder. His eyes were glued to the instrument board. In 45 minutes we had pulled through the upper layers of clouds into a brilliant sunshine with mountain peaks towering on each side.

I had heard of blind flying, but this was my first real experience, and I was relieved at being out in the sunshine again. We flew on another thirty minutes and I sighted the top of a pyramid projecting through the clouds. After passing this point Snyder put the ship into a glide to enter the clouds. All of a sudden we came through the lower level, and followed some high tension wires for about five minutes.

Eddie seemed very much at ease, but I had been figuring that if I ever got out of this flight alive, I would head north! No more Mexican flying for me! We did not land at Mexico City due to the heavy fog, but turned and flew back to Tampico with our passengers and mail.

We were in the air approximately five hours and I had made my first flight over the "Hump" without ever getting a glimpse of Mexico City. I had learned plenty about blind flying, and my thoughts of being able to do this myself were dispelled later when such trips became a frequent occurrence.

This experience in Mexico was probably the greatest a pilot could ever hope to have in those days, and only a few pilots ventured to gain it. Flying the Atlantic was comparatively easy, and it was through experiences over this country that I later became fitted for that ocean hop. I firmly believe that my flight to England during October of 1930 under nearly impossible weather conditions would probably have terminated in the middle of the Atlantic, had I not had this valuable experience.

When Pan American took effective control of Mexicana the following year, 1929, the Tampico to Mexico City route was one of the most challenging with its mountainous terrain, dangerous passes and frequent thunderstorms. While only some 200 miles in length, it required a two-day rail journey. Pan American would later introduce the more reliable tri-motored Fokker and Ford monoplanes to the route as well as pilots who had been given special training in blind or instrument flying.

Before these developments, however, Erroll Boyd was placed in charge of operations from Mexicana's new base in Merida in the Yucatan Peninsula. Early flights for the young company took more than five hours of flying time over plenty of jungle on the route to Vera Cruz, handled by Boyd and three other pilots.

In early 1929 Mrs. Boyd and two of their daughters joined Erroll in a beautiful home in Merida provided by the company. Mrs. Boyd was unhappy there, however, claiming that it was a man's country, unsuitable for raising young children. After three months in Merida, Erroll resigned due to the pleading of his wife and sailed with them back to New York. There, Erroll would soon land another flying job with a promising company.

11

Flying with Accident-Prone Coastal Airways

ERROLL BOYD arrived back in New York City in February 1929 and soon landed a good job with Coastal Airways of New York City. Although it was just prior to the stock market crash of October 1929, an air of optimism prevailed during the dying days of the roaring twenties. Any airline conceived at this time was thought to have both growth potential and great expectations. Coastal Airways and its plans to fly from New York to the state capital, Albany, 150 miles up the Hudson River, seemed a sure-fire proposition.

Coastal Airways was an outgrowth of Atlantic Airways, a small amphibious operation, and Mill Basin Aircraft, a seaplane operator based on an inlet of Jamaica Bay in the southeast section of Brooklyn. Its organizers were F.W. Dalrymple and Ezio De Angelis.

The company originally had three Curtiss Seagull flying boats, and then two Loening amphibians. In 1929 it acquired seven new Fairchild 71 Wasp-powered cabin seaplanes. On delivery of the first six-passenger Fairchild, Coastal inaugurated a daily seaplane service from New York to Albany with two trips in each direction. The company would later fly to Norfolk, Va. and Washington, D.C., in addition to charter flights and some float training.

Northbound passengers from New York boarded a speedboat at the end of 42nd Street and were whisked up the East River to North Beach (now LaGuardia Airport), where they transferred to a waiting Fairchild. The passengers enjoyed a scenic flight up the beautiful Hudson River, sometimes termed "The Rhine of America." After a flight of one hour and twenty-five minutes the pilot would land and taxi to the dock within easy walking distance of downtown Albany. The cost of the journey: $17.50 one-way or $33.50 for the round trip.

A brochure on the Albany-New York route described points of interest:

> The propeller hums . . . the spray dashes in rapid
> rhythm against cabin windows . . . three States unfolding
> beneath us, jewelled with lakes . . . the Gothic Halls of
> Vasar appear like doll houses . . . beneath us a train creeps
> like a toy among the hills . . . infinitesimal cars crawl along
> the filaments of roads . . . over the esplanade and parade
> ground of West Point where the cadet squads move like
> dice upon a back-gammon board . . . specks upon the
> water become magnified . . . we are descending.

The brochure ends: "Save time to and from airports. Fly the over-water way."

Later in the summer Coastal's Fairchilds were flown to Lake George and to Saratoga Springs for the famous month of horse racing in August. For the first time a sporting New Yorker could fly to the races at Saratoga and be home before dark.

Coastal nevertheless suffered setbacks. President Dalrymple, who had no licence, experienced a low-altitude spin at North Beach and dropped a Curtiss Seagull into Flushing Bay on May 25, 1929. He survived but the plane was a washout.

Erroll Boyd reported that several operational accidents took place which brought into question the safety of Coastal's operations. Cliff McMillan, "breaking every rule in the book," flew under the bridge at Poughkeepsie during the boat races. With glassy water making it difficult to judge the height, he flew into the river with full power on. The pontoons and engine were ripped off, and five passengers seriously injured. A few days later Guy McLaughlin landed a Fairchild in Jamaica Bay in a fog and hit a sandbar off Barren Island. The aircraft's tail was twisted off during salvage operations.

While both Peter Talbot and Erroll Boyd were listed as operations managers of Coastal Airways in 1929, Boyd probably took over the post early in the summer.

Operations went better during July and August. On the Saturday after Labour Day, however, veteran Coastal Airways pilot William H.

Alexander, after dropping off his Albany passengers at North Beach, was heading for the Mill Basin home base when he ran into thick fog down the East River. Too late he saw his planned emergency landing path at Coney Island crowded with sun worshippers and bathers. He hit a "deep water" sign which caused the seaplane to swerve toward the beach and flip over in the midst of holiday-makers. Two children were instantly killed and many others injured.

Only one day after the Coney Island accident, pilot Henry "Hank" Ramsdell in another Fairchild taxied out of the Mill Basin terminal "to fetch operations manager Erroll Boyd from his hotel in Rockaway Park." He was taxiing fast or flying low over Jamaica Bay through wisps of fog when he hit a fishing boat, killing one occupant and injuring another. The tabloids of New York listed it as "the first case of a hit-and-run airplane."

The authorities initially thought Boyd was in the aircraft at the time of the accident, so Erroll spent most of Sunday and Monday in the hoosegow in Jamaica with Hank, who thought he had hit a submerged log. Dozens of times Hank Ramsdell said over and over in his Louisiana drawl, "I never hit no boat." Subsequently the paint on the gunnel of the boat was found to be the same as that on the plane's pontoon.

The investigating district attorney for Brooklyn was William O'Dwyer, later mayor of New York City. Boyd took O'Dwyer in a similar aircraft to prove that it was impossible for Ramsdell to see a small fishing boat ahead of him unless he were up on the "step" which was quite impossible due to the foggy weather at the time. Ramsdell was released from jail and placed on probation for one year.

Following Coastal Airways' major accidents, Frank Tichner, editor and publisher of *Aero Digest*, the "mouthpiece" of aviation, sent for Boyd with the intent of putting an end to the company's operations. With all Coastal's recent flights to Albany, Norfolk and Washington plus many charter flights, Boyd believed the company flew more passengers during this short period than any other scheduled U.S. airline at that time. To put this operation in perspective, combined transcontinental air-rail service – rail by night, Ford tri-motor by day – had begun only in July 1929 offering a forty-eight hour schedule which carried a mere 153 passengers in its first month.

When Boyd saw Tichner, he found that the publisher had also called in famed stunt and test pilot, Al Williams, evidently in an advisory capacity. Williams had his popular corn cobb pipe perched upside down between pursed lips. Boyd felt Tichner's intentions were to write an editorial which would mean curtains for Coastal. He bluntly asked Boyd his experience in operating an airline.

Boyd produced his log book showing over 4,000 hours of difficult and safe flying. Tichner queried the company's selection of pilots. Boyd told him that Alexander, McMillan, McLaughlin and Ramsdell were issued their transport licences by the Civil Aviation Authority (CAA), and were considered among the more experienced fliers in the country.

In so many words Tichner told Boyd Coastal could continue as long as Boyd did most of the flying. The threat of the printed word by Tichner and public opinion gave Boyd no choice but to discharge the four accident-prone pilots. For the next month Boyd made at least two round trips to Albany a day.

In 1929 Coastal Airways was chartered by president Dorman of Acme Films to look for Lindbergh, who was off on his honeymoon in a small motor cruiser, presumably heading for Cape Cod. In Bridgeport, Connecticut, Dorman and Boyd encountered dozens of newspaper reporters detailed to secure the same story.

Dorman thought that Lindy had headed out to sea and prevailed upon Boyd to fly out and look for them. Out about 100 miles Boyd convinced Dorman that the famous couple were not out that far. This reminded Boyd of the late Russell Boardman during his bootleg activities. Boardman would hire pilots to fly out to the twelve-mile limit on the pretext of taking pictures of Rum Row, when actually they were dropping messages in bottles giving instructions for the landing of whiskey that night!

Later that same day they found Lindbergh moored in Cape Cod Canal. They flew down as close as possible, took pictures and waved at Lindbergh, who waved back. At dusk Boyd quickly flew back to New York. The scoop was of such magnitude and the pictures so good that Erroll was given a $500 bonus for the flying job.

Faced with accidents, pending lawsuits, aircraft repair bills and payments on the rest of the fleet, Coastal Airways was approaching bankruptcy. In August Ezio De Angelis, who had succeeded Dalrymple as president, announced that Coastal Airways soon would be merging with Airvia Transportation Company, Inc., and would then have a combined fleet of eighteen aircraft. An exchange of stock of the two companies was being arranged. Boyd had no part in these plans.

Airvia had established seaplane service between New York and Boston on July 22 with two Savoia-Marchetti S-55s. Airvia had reaped a great deal of publicity as sponsors of the transatlantic flight of Roger Q. Williams and Lewis A. Yancey on July 8-9, 1929. Flying from Old Orchard, Maine to Santander in Spain and then on to Rome, Williams and Yancey were much in the news. A year later Williams would make a record non-stop flight from New York to Bermuda and back with Erroll Boyd.

Airvia had announced great plans to fly to Montreal, Palm Beach, Nassau, Havana and Bermuda. Some 35,000 shares of Airvia stock had already been peddled at an average of $10 per share, most being sold illegally through the mail. Although the stock manipulators were forced to surrender to authorities in late August, Airvia as a company was finished. Guilty by association and unable to keep its promises, Coastal Airways floundered in shallow waters.

The onset of the depression and the stock market crash were the final nails in its coffin. By February 1930 Fairchild Airplane and Engine Corporation had repossessed the last of the Model 71s that Coastal had acquired. It is interesting to note that one Fairchild on floats went to Canada's Department of National Defence and three others went to service with Pacific Alaska Airways, Pan Am's far north subsidiary.

When Coastal Airways folded, Erroll Boyd was once again left looking for a job. He soon found one with the controversial and affluent Charles A. Levine.

12

The Columbia, a Very Famous Aircraft

THE BELLANCA MONOPLANE, *Columbia* or *Maple Leaf*, in which Erroll Boyd flew the Atlantic, became the most famous aircraft of its era based on its many record flights. Not only was the *Columbia* the first airplane to cross the Atlantic twice, but it also established remarkable endurance and efficiency records.

Its designer, Giuseppe M. Bellanca, was one of the early great aviation pioneers. Born in 1886 in the Sicilian village of Sciacca, Italy, high on a hilltop overlooking the Mediterranean, Bellanca described it as a perfect place for kite flying and for observing air in motion and its effect on seagulls. He obtained a degree in engineering in Milan and became professor of industrial mathematics at its Royal Institute.

Young Bellanca first became interested in aviation in 1906, only three years after the little-publicized flight of the Wright brothers. In collaboration with two others he completed the building of a two-seat pusher biplane in 1909. Later that year he designed his first tractor biplane which was flown at Taliedo, Italy, in 1910.

In 1911 the Bellanca family came to America and settled in Brooklyn, where this soft-spoken man was viewed as a foreigner with strange ideas. His first American creation was a parasol-wing monoplane with an air-cooled thirty hp Anzani motor, completed with his family's help in the back of his brother's grocery store.

Many people said at this time that if God had wanted man to fly, he would have given him wings. Bellanca replied that perhaps God had given him a brain to devise wings. With his new plane Bellanca taught himself to fly at Mineola, Long Island. At first he only flew carefully in very short, straight hops, but he soon learned to bank and circle.

In September 1912 he formed the Bellanca Aeroplane Company and Flying School. Free legal counsel was provided by a cherubic lawyer named Fiorello H. LaGuardia, later renowned as the irrepressible mayor of New York City.

The operation continued through 1915 and a few planes were built as needed. LaGuardia, who had just purchased a Model T Ford, offered to teach Bellanca to drive in return for flying lessons. On the early flying machine the pilot sat on a sort of bird perch behind the motor which would often spatter the pilot with hot oil.

In 1916 Bellanca became consulting engineer for the Maryland Pressed Steel Company for whom he designed and built several small but very efficient aircraft. In 1919 Clarence Chamberlain, a wartime flying instructor who was later to become famous, ordered the first model of a Bellanca C.E. sport biplane powered by a forty-five hp motor. He flew 220 miles from Garden City, Long Island, to Glen Falls, N.Y., in the fast time of two hours and five minutes.

"I was to find out frequently in my later acquaintance with Mr. Bellanca that, unlike many designers, his estimates usually were conservative about what his ship would do, rather than over-optimistic," said Chamberlain, who later flew the Atlantic two weeks after Lindbergh.

The Maryland company decided to get out of the aviation business in the quiet postwar period. In 1921 Victor Roos of Omaha, Nebraska, negotiated to take over its aviation assets, forming the Roos-Bellanca company in Omaha. Bellanca moved west. In 1922 and 1923 his newly-designed C.F. aircraft with its ninety hp Anzani engine won nearly all prizes in efficiency contests in Monmouth, Illinois, and St. Louis, Missouri, as well as a racing trophy at Detroit.

Bellanca's model C.F. became the first successful cabin monoplane manufactured in the U.S. It was a forerunner of future air transports. Its historic significance was recognized by 1980 when this most efficient aircraft of its day was restored like new at the Smithsonian Institute's Garber facility in Washington.

Sadly, this great design of a $5,000 cabin monoplane was not a commercial success in spite of its great performance, mainly because

THE FAMOUS MONOPLANE "COLUMBIA"

RECORD OF THE FAMOUS MONOPLANE "COLUMBIA

1925: Designed by Guiseppi M. Bellanca, built by the Wright Aeronautical Corp., Paterson, N.J. Wing spread 46'6" – Wing surface 272 sq. ft. Length 26'9". Weight empty 1850 lbs. – Gas capacity 502 gal. Oil capacity 27 gal. – Power plant 220 H.P. Wright Whirlwind Engine.

1926: Won the all efficiency contest National Air Races, Philadelphia Sesquincentennial, Lieut. C.C. Champion, Pilot.

1927: World's long distance non-stop record Roosevelt Field, Long island, N.Y. to Eisleben, Germany, 3911 miles – time 42 hrs. 25 mins. Clarence Chamberlain, Pilot – Charles Levine, passenger.

1927: World's record non-stop endurance flight, Roosevelt Field, Long island, N.Y. 51 hrs. 11 min. Bert Acosta and Clarence Chamberlin, Pilots. May 14.

1928: World Record Non-stop flight, New York to Havana, Cuba. Pilot Wilmer Stultz, O. Le Boutilier, Navigator – Mable Bole, Passenger.

1929: Flight New York to Cailifornia. Comdr. John Iseman, U.S.N. Pilot. Lieut. J. Farnum, Co-pilot. Racing number changed from 140 to 185 – came in second.

1930: June 29 – First non-stop world record flight New York to Bermuda and return – time 17 hrs. 3 mins. Erroll Boyd – Roger Q. Williams, Pilots. Harry P. Connor, Navigator. Racing number changed back to 140.

1930: October 9 – Second trans-Atlantic flight Toronto, Canada to London, England – official government air mail to Europe. Erroll Boyd, Pilot – Harry P. Connor, Navigator. Distance 3740 Statute miles – elapsed time 36 hrs. 10 min.

1933: June 11 – First non-stop flight New York to Haiti, Erroll Boyd, Pilot – Robert G. Lyon, Co-Pilot – H.P. Davis, Passenger. Distance 2379 miles – elapsed time 24 hrs. 8 mins.

1933: June 7 – Port Au Prince, Haiti to Wasington, D.C. Carrying special new stamp issue. Erroll Boyd, Pilot – Robert Lyon, Co-Pilot.

1934: Destroyed by fire at Ballanca factory, Newscastle, Delaware.

Columbia (Courtesy of Boyd family)

the market was flooded with many wartime surplus aircraft selling as low as $250.

In late 1923 Bellanca resigned from the Roos venture and re-formed his own company in the former Lawrence Sperry factory at Farmingdale, Long Island. Business was slow but he rebuilt three Liberty-powered de Havilland 4 mailplanes for the night mail service between Chicago and Cheyenne, Wyoming, using the high-lift Bellanca wing and bracing, a modification the airmail pilots praised highly.

Through contacts made by his friend, company test pilot Clarence Chamberlain, Bellanca joined the Wright Aeronautical Corporation in 1925 at Paterson, New Jersey, as consulting engineer in charge of aeroplane construction. The Wright people were looking for a modern monoplane seating four to six passengers which would demonstrate the efficiency of their 200 hp nine-cylinder J-4 Whirlwind air-cooled engine.

The resulting Wright-Bellanca WB-1, first flown in September 1925, won speed and efficiency events at the New York races the following month. Early in 1926, being groomed for an attack on the world's endurance record, the overloaded WB-1 flown by Fred Becker was wiped out during a hard landing on a gusty day.

Even before the crash the Wright company had a second prototype under construction. Instead of an all-wood airframe, the WB-2, later to be christened the *Columbia*, featured a new fabric-covered steel-tube fuselage and the newer J-5 engine. The profile remained essentially unchanged.

While reliable airplane structures had been built toward the end of World War I, the appearance of the Wright J-5 in 1926 marked a comparable milestone in powerplants. In retrospect, it was the first mating of almost total reliability in an engine-and-airframe combination in one airplane.

The WB-2 made its debut at Philadelphia during the 1926 National Air Races. The Wright-Bellanca entry easily won the efficiency race well ahead of Walter Beech's new Travel Air. Distant third was a new Buhl Airster flown by sportsman pilot Henry B. duPont.

Bellanca's prestige was further enhanced when it won the Detroit News Trophy efficiency contest which drew such entries as the new

Ford tri-motor, Buhl and Pitcairn. The WB-2 hefted a load of 1607 pounds – the equivalent of nine passengers – at an average of 121 mph.

Wright Aero then abandoned plans for aircraft production as the WB-2's Whirlwind engine had proved itself. As the company had established itself as a world leader in the power plant field, its officers felt it would be bad for business to compete with its own engine customers. The Wright company decided to sell the plane to the highest bidder and advised G.M. Bellanca that his services were no longer required, although he retained the design rights.

Bellanca considered some new affiliations such as with T. Claude Ryan of San Diego (builder of the *Spirit of St. Louis*) and Walter Beech of Wichita but decided to cast his lot with a young Brooklyn wheeler-dealer named Charlie Levine. A millionaire at age twenty-eight, Levine had made money by buying surplus shell casings and ammunition and later selling them back to the government at enormous profits. Levine, whose father had been a successful scrap-metal dealer, promised to finance production of the WB-2 in a new factory, a promise not kept. He also would play an important role in Erroll Boyd's aviation career.

The Columbia Aircraft Corporation was formed in December 1926, with Levine as chairman and G.M. Bellanca as president. Levine purchased the WB-2 from Wright Aero for $15,500 in early 1927. It came with special cabin fuel tanks built for an endurance flight which the Wright company had planned.

The next challenge was to break the world endurance record of forty-five hours held by Maurice Drouhin and Jean Landry of France. Clarence Chamberlain agreed to stay on as pilot of the WB-2 for the new company. Levine brought in Lieutenant Leigh Wade, one of the round-the-world 1924 army fliers, for added publicity value. Personality differences soon surfaced – a common occurrence around Levine – and Wade quit. His replacement was the burly and colourful Bert Acosta.

Many "experts" predicted that Chamberlain and Acosta would crash on take-off. That was the fate of Rene Fonck, French war hero, while attempting to be first between New York and Paris in September, 1926, in the Sikorsky S-35 trimotor biplane. One Curtiss engineer estimated before take-off that, with the load she carried for the endurance flight, the Bellanca's ceiling was 600 feet below sea level!

The Bellanca fooled them. She took off from Roosevelt Field, Long Island on April 12, 1927, with a run of only 1,200 feet, less than a quarter of the distance available, which even surprised Chamberlain and Acosta. She established a new world endurance record of fifty-one hours and eleven minutes, exceeding the previous one by six hours!

This was the same plane Erroll Boyd eventually would acquire, and the one that Charles Lindbergh tried unsuccessfully to purchase.

13

Lindbergh's Attempt to Buy the **Columbia**

IN A CEREMONY on April 24, 1927, the WB-2 was christened the *Columbia* by Levine's eight-year-old daughter, Ardith, with a bottle of ginger ale as this was the prohibition era. On this very same day Chamberlain averted a serious accident by landing successfully on one wheel when a fitting broke on one main gear leg. Levine's daughter and a young friend were on board, but unhurt.

The aircraft had proven her capability to fly to Europe nonstop. But Charles Lindbergh would gain most of the glory when he alone in his Ryan monoplane *Spirit of St. Louis* took off from Roosevelt field on May 20 arriving in Paris 33^1/$_2$ hours later winning the $25,000 Orteig prize. In the previous year the race for the prize had claimed six lives.

Earlier the *Columbia* almost became Lindbergh's plane. He had great respect for its designer and described the Bellancas as the world's most efficient aircraft. His negotiations to purchase it from the Wright company had been unsuccessful as the firm was not enthusiastic about a single pilot endeavor with possible adverse publicity in the event of failure.

Lindbergh then had approached Levine, who offered to sell him the *Columbia*. Lindbergh returned to his St. Louis sponsors and came back in February, 1927, with a cheque for $15,000 to close the deal. Levine then added a new stipulation that the Columbia Aircraft Corporation must reserve the right to select the crew.

In declining, the chagrined Lindbergh said: "We would be paying a considerable sum just for the privilege of painting St. Louis on the side of the fuselage."

Lindbergh was driven away to the Ryan company in San Diego where the *Spirit of St. Louis* was built quickly. It was also powered by the same reliable Wright J-5 engine.

Selection of the crew had also delayed the *Columbia's* transatlantic attempt. Charles Levine wanted a more dashing publicity-oriented pilot than the quiet, conservative teetotaller, Clarence Chamberlain. But the plane's designer, Giuseppe Bellanca, insisted on the experienced Chamberlain who knew the plane so well. When Chamberlain, pilot Lloyd Bertaud and Levine could not agree on flight details, and a legal action by Bertaud – who was being dropped from the crew – caused further delay, Lindbergh was allowed to scoop them.

The *Columbia* finally got away on June 4, two weeks after Lindbergh, with pilot Chamberlain and passenger Levine on board. Levine had jumped on at the very last moment because his wife, Grace, had refused to concur with the hazardous flight. Some forty-three hours later they landed not far from Berlin, Germany, having set a new distance record. Unlike the *Spirit of St. Louis*, the *Columbia* had been designed as a regular commercial aircraft.

Toward the end of its first transatlantic flight the *Columbia* was forced up to about 20,000 feet because of inclement weather. Just before daylight the aircraft stalled and went into a spiral dive. The balanced rudder, oscillating in the terrific dive, whipped the rudder bar back and forth and shook the rear end of the plane. The airspeed indicator had passed its maximum calibrated mark of 160 mph.

Chamberlain, who had dozed off while Levine was flying level, finally got the aircraft under control at 4,000 feet. The *Columbia* had proven itself to be a very sturdy aircraft, able to withstand great forces during a very rapid, unplanned descent of some 16,000 feet.

When Clarence Chamberlain took over the controls from Levine during the uncontrolled descent, Charlie laughed and showed no concern. He was obviously suffering from lack of oxygen or anoxia, about which little was known in that era.

The *Columbia* also survived an unusual trip from Paris to London later that summer, flown solo by Charles Levine who was not a qualified pilot. He had had a few lessons much earlier from Bert Acosta, but had never soloed. After the record crossing from New York to Germany with Clarence Chamberlain, Levine wanted to attempt an east-west crossing but Chamberlain wanted no part of it.

Not a man to accept no for an answer, Levine hired Maurice

Drouhin, the renowned French flier. The papers began to hint that Charlie and his pilot weren't hitting it off and that Drouhin had hired lawyers to protect his interests.

More than lawyers were needed to thwart Levine. Lunching with Drouhin and others, Levine excused himself to go to the washroom and fled to the airport to take the *Columbia* out of French jurisdiction. He was carrying the armature of the magneto in his pocket as a precaution against someone making off with the plane. Flashing the armature to the gendarmes guarding the aircraft, he told them he would just warm up the motor to see it was well.

Instead, he made a hazardous takeoff. His canny plan was to follow an airliner to London's airport at Croydon, but he ended up following one bound for Amsterdam. Realizing his mistake, he turned back and had the luck to pick up a Croydon-bound transport. An hour and a half later he was over Croydon – all over Croydon. Word of his escapade had been flashed from Paris, and ambulances and fire trucks had been alerted.

After two unsuccessful attempts to land when he bounced high and reapplied power, the authorities sent up a plane to try to guide him down. On his third try he bounced the aircraft onto the airport and stopped a few feet from its boundary.

One press report said the first official to arrive yelled: "What are you trying to do?"

"Oh, hello," said Levine. "I think I need a shave."

"Wasn't the one you just had close enough?" rasped the official.

In England, Levine was reported to have shaken off his friend, heiress Mabel Boll, and hired Captain Hinchcliffe, a World War I hero, to fly him to India. They got only as far as Rome where Charlie continued to make headlines. Dropping a present over the palace for dictator Benito Mussolini's son, they were fired upon by the guards who thought the plane was dropping a bomb.

Back in America, the quiet Guiseppe Bellanca, disenchanted with Levine, had severed his connections in mid-1927 with the Columbia Aircraft Corporation. The company was supposed to build WB-2 monoplanes for use on the New York to Chicago airmail route, upon which Levine had bid before he came under investigation by the Justice Department for other contract irregularities. Bellanca concluded he would be better off looking elsewhere for financial backing.

A small man of innate dignity and integrity, Bellanca was discovering that calculating stress loads and devising efficient airfoils were easier for him than understanding human relations. His unfortunate relation with Charles Levine was only a temporary setback because the Bellanca Aircraft Corporation went on to build some great aircraft of which the C.F. and WB-2 *Columbia* were forerunners.

The *Columbia* continued to establish records. This most famous of the Bellanca planes made the first nonstop flight from New York to Havana in 1928. Its pilot was Wilbur Stultz, its passenger, socialite Mabel Boll, known as the Queen of Diamonds. Wilbur Stultz made more headlines later that same year when he piloted the Fokker tri-motored seaplane *Friendship* to Europe along with Louis Gordon and Amelia Earhart, who became the first woman to cross the Atlantic by airplane. They took twenty hours and forty minutes from Trepassey Bay, Newfoundland, to Burry Port, Wales.

In September 1929 Bellanca Aircraft of Canada was organized with sales and manufacturing rights for Bellanca products. A number of Bellanca Pacemakers, a later development from the Columbia-type, were produced at Canadian Vickers, Montreal. Many were used by the Department of National Defence for photographic and transport work and for Commercial Airways that operated the mail between Edmonton and Aklavik, 1,800 miles down the Mackenzie River to the Arctic Ocean.

One of the early Bellanca CH-300 Pacemakers, powered originally by a 300 hp Wright J-6-9 engine but now with a more powerful Pratt & Whitney Wasp Jr., is on display in Canada's national aviation museum at Rockliffe Airport in Ottawa. Built in 1929 and sold to the museum in 1964 after twenty-eight years of active bush flying, it is one of the few existing specimens of this outstanding aircraft family.

John Heinmuller, in his 1945 *Chronology of Aviation*, wrote that the *Columbia* was "probably the greatest of her time (1925-1934) and certainly one that outperformed any other single aircraft." Others have described it as the "father" of the modern closed-cabin airliner.

Giuseppe Bellanca, whom Erroll Boyd greatly respected, died in 1960, the same year as Boyd, after devoting his entire life to aviation progress. Like the *Columbia*, his planes were firmly built and highly efficient. They could lift more weight per horsepower than competitive planes because of Bellanca's philosophy of design that every possible part of the aeroplane in flight should lift its own weight. A likable, mild-mannered man, his outstanding contributions to aeronautics are legend.

Charles Lindbergh met Bellanca in late 1926 during his search for a transatlantic aircraft, and later said of him: "One feels, in his presence, genius, capability, confidence . . . what he says, you can believe."

As for artifacts from the *Columbia*, very few remain because of the almost complete destruction of the aircraft in a fire at the Bellanca factory in Newcastle, Delaware, on January 25, 1934. The aircraft door was maintained as a souvenir for many years by Erroll Boyd's good friend, Major M.K. Lee, on his farm at Cornwall, Connecticut. The $12 second-hand wooden propeller that pulled Boyd across the Atlantic is unlocated although it was once on display at the Wings Club in New York. Models of the aircraft are on display at the national aviation museums in Ottawa and Washington. The latter also has a souvenir aluminum ashtray made from the metal of the fuel tank of the *Columbia*, greatest aircraft of its era.

14

Record-Breaking Bermuda Flight

EARLY IN the new decade Erroll Boyd would be involved in a record-breaking Bermuda flight. In December 1929 he gained employment with the eccentric millionaire, Charles Levine, who was building some airplanes in Long Island City. Erroll was placed on the payroll along with such noted pilots as Roger Q. Williams, Burr Leyson, Bert Acosta and Commander John Wycliff Iseman.

Bert Acosta developed the reputation as an authentic giant in the early flying days but was also described as the bad boy of aviation because of his off-duty drinking adventures and matrimonial and financial problems. He was an instructor at the Curtiss school in Toronto early in World War I and had set a speed record of nearly 200 mph in 1921.

His most publicized flight was as Commander Richard Byrd's pilot along with Arctic pioneer Bernt Balchen as co-pilot in the Fokker *America*, the first transport-type plane to cross the Atlantic six weeks after Lindbergh's epic 1927 flight. He could have beat Lindbergh because, at one time, he contemplated a solo transatlantic flight in the *Columbia* until Charlie Levine decided otherwise.

Bert Acosta ended his latter days in the charity ward of a tuberculosis hospital in Denver where Erroll Boyd used to correspond with him. He died in 1959. One of his crew members on his transatlantic flight, Commander George Noville, scattered his ashes into the Pacific Ocean. Aircraft designer Vincent Burnelli said he had a born instinct for flying just like a great violinist or pianist has for his instrument.

John Iseman had flown the *Columbia* to a second-place finish in a

New York-Los Angeles derby in 1928, won by Art Goebel flying a Lockheed Vega. Goebel previously had won the controversial Dole competition to Hawaii.

Boyd and these pioneer pilots employed by Levine were paid $200 per week, an exceptionally good salary for that era. Boyd surmised correctly that Charlie Levine enjoyed being surrounded by pilots. Basking in the reflected publicity gratified his vanity. The piloting job in 1930, however, was not without its risks, and a close fraternity developed among these early airmen.

Burr Leyson and Boyd were in a bar on 42nd Street when the news came over the radio that Wilmer Stultz had been killed in a crash at Roosevelt Field, thus ending the career of one of the *Columbia's* earliest pilots. Stultz flew it on the first nonstop flight from New York to Havana in 1928 with O. LeBoutilier as navigator and with passenger, Mabel Boll, a Rochester heiress known as the Queen of Diamonds in the entertainment world. In that same year Stultz flew Amelia Earhart as the first female transatlantic aircraft passenger. Four years later Amelia would make her epic solo crossing from Newfoundland.

Mabel Boll was also one of Charlie Levine's big publicity attractions. Boyd recalled flying both of them to Detroit one time when, passing over Syracuse in a snowstorm, he decided to descend for an enroute landing and hold. The temperamental Mabel, sitting in the rear of the four-place aircraft, had other ideas. She hit Boyd over the head with a large alligator bag opening a cut on the side of his face. This, however, did not stop Boyd from landing and holding until the next morning when the weather was clear and cold.

One headline at this time publicized the crash of Jack Ashcroft and Viola Gentry who were attempting to set a new world endurance record. Ashcroft was killed and Gentry was hospitalized for a year in a plaster cast. Gentry was a friend of the Boyds for many years.

By May 1, 1930, Boyd had accumulated 6,575 flying hours. In the summer of this year he teamed with Roger Q. Williams and Harry Connor to make a record-breaking flight in the *Columbia* from New York to Bermuda and back. Williams was already famous for having made the first flight from America to Rome via Spain in 1929. Lieutenant Harry Connor was an experienced navigation officer with the U.S. Navy. As a young man Boyd had spent a winter in Bermuda prior to the outbreak of World War I, and was familiar with the British colony.

The original plan was to fly to Bermuda, spend a day there, and return the third day. As Connor later wrote in *Aero Digest*: "We aimed to bring out the fact that this beautiful coral island, a paradise for vacationists all the year 'round, can become really a close neighbour . . . Two days of travel each way are required by steamer, but we knew that to fly would take less than eight hours."

As no suitable place for landing and take-off existed in Bermuda, the team decided upon a nonstop return flight as the best means of establishing the feasibility of tourist travel to the island by air. Much needed to be learned of flight conditions and navigational methods before regular service could be considered seriously. Their aim was to apply scientific navigation to aircraft over the ocean.

Williams, Boyd and Connor took off from Roosevelt Field on their seventeen-hour return flight at 5:01 a.m. on Sunday, June 29, 1930. Dr. Kimball, meteorologist of the New York weather bureau, advised them to expect good weather except for showers and overcast skies around Bermuda in the early afternoon. They had planned to get away at 2:00 a.m. but were delayed three hours "because of the condition of the field and light variable winds." They carried no radio, since radios at that time were primitive, heavy and short-range. Some people at the airport had placed bets at five to one that they would never return!

Exactly on the navigator's estimate, they circled the northbound *S.S. Fort St. George* and then headed directly over her fore-and-aft line to check their compasses and drift.

"The passengers in their summer attire were running about the deck," Boyd later wrote, "frantically waving pieces of apparel to show their delight at seeing a tiny airplane so far out in the Atlantic Ocean."

They later passed abeam of the motor ship *Bermuda*. By early afternoon Boyd had stripped down to his underwear due to the motor heat and outside temperature. They were down to 400 feet as they neared Bermuda and the deteriorating weather. As they flew through a tropical downpour, their left magneto drowned out making an emergency landing a definite possibility if and when they reached Bermuda. But where?

From his knowledge of Bermuda, Boyd thought of the golf course, made out of coral rock, with its bunkers, sand traps and rolling terrain – a sure place for a crack-up.

"Connor calculated we should arrive over the islands at 2:10 p.m.;

and I had great confidence in his judgment, but at 2:10 there was no Bermuda in sight, and I became quite worried and thought to myself that we may have missed the islands entirely . . . I knew that Connor could no more navigate since he had no sun to shoot at," Boyd said.

"I was a little suspicious when Harry sent up word to change course, stating we would arrive over Bermuda in ten minutes . . . However, at 2:23 we sighted the islands. The motor was missing badly because of the drenching rain . . . I was doing the flying, Williams was busy writing notes, and Connor had a grin from ear to ear. This slim calculating naval officer had accomplished a navigational feat second to none."

Connor later wrote that they arrived over the Hamilton harbour in a heavy downpour with visibility of less than half a mile. They were then flying at altitudes of between fifty and 150 feet and made a complete circle of the island.

At 2:43 p.m. Roger Williams dropped the mail sack at Woodland where it was retrieved by Harold Aitken, chief engineer of the Hotel Bermudiana. Then they set course for New York at 2:44 rather than risking an emergency landing. If the one good magneto would hold out, they soon would be in the sunshine which would dry out the dead magneto.

The remainder of the trip was fairly routine. The sun set about 8:30 p.m. and they climbed to 2,500 feet as a safety precaution for night flying. When their sea passage ended, they made a bee-line for Roosevelt Field. The visibility was then less than five miles and some fog was rolling in from the sea. They could not see the lights clearly at Roosevelt Field where a crowd of 1,000 awaited them. They landed instead at nearby Valley Stream at 10:03 p.m. after a flight of just over seventeen hours.

In summary, their average ground speed southbound was seventy-two knots or eight-three miles per hour, and northbound ninety-four knots or 108 mph. Average fuel consumption southbound was twelve gallons per hour, and northbound fourteen gallons per hour. On landing they had ten hours of fuel remaining.

About this trip Erroll Boyd wrote much later: "The flight placed before the world another 'first' in aviation history, not for Williams or myself, but alone for Harry P. Connor who had proved his exceptional ability as an aerial navigator."

Two other flights in this era attempted the Bermuda flight. On

January 4, 1931, William S. McLaren and Mrs. Beryl Hart took off from North Beach, Queens, New York in the float-equipped Bellanca monoplane *Tradewind* for Paris with planned landings at Bermuda and the Azores. While seen on course by three ships more than halfway to Bermuda, the aircraft never arrived. Early the previous year William Alexander flew the route to Bermuda but was forced to land on the sea short of his goal. He took off the next morning and completed the flight. He was accompanied by Lewis Yancey, navigator, and Zleh Bouck, radio operator.

Following in the footsteps of the pioneers, both Pan American and Imperial Airways inaugurated regular mail and passenger service between New York and Bermuda in the summer of 1937 using Sikorsky and Short flying boats. Regular air service became established seven years after Boyd's pioneering flight, fulfilling a project he had mentioned while interned in Holland during the First World War.

15

Transatlantic Preparations

THE HISTORY-MAKING flight to Bermuda in the summer of 1930 gave Erroll Boyd complete confidence in the Columbia as the aircraft for his solo flight to Europe. Charlie Levine had already promised Boyd the plane for the flight.

Knowing Charlie's changeable nature, eccentricities and love of publicity, Boyd had a plan to confirm the deal. He arrived in the offices of Columbia Airlines in Long Island City, New York, with two editors from the *Morning Telegraph*, Sloan Taylor (a former flier) and Paul Jeans, in order to have witnesses to Levine's confirmation of the flight.

On the day following the interview, Levine was pleased with the morning headlines. The publicity stunt had worked. Boyd's long cherished dream was nearing reality.

Fourteen years earlier when Boyd was interned in Holland, Joseph J. O'Neill of the *New York World* had written about the Canadian's ambition to do what England's Lieut. John Cyril Porte had planned prior to the outbreak of war in 1914 – to fly across the Atlantic Ocean. Boyd again was making plans to do it in 1919 and was expecting to leave for Newfoundland in mid-June of that year.

In May of 1919, however, no fewer than five British teams were in St. John's, Newfoundland, preparing for a non-stop transatlantic flight. Most plans were dropped when Alcock and Brown's prize-winning flight took place on June 14-15.

And now to return to 1930. While Charlie Levine's behaviour and financial dealings got him into considerable trouble in the next few years, Boyd's major reason in accepting a job with him was to secure the *Columbia* for a transatlantic flight. Most of the public in this era looked upon pilots and their financial backers as reckless and foolhardy.

At this time Roger Q. Williams and Erroll Boyd were doing much of the test flying for Levine's Columbia Airlines, perhaps better described as an aircraft company. The ambitious Levine was building a plane called *Uncle Sam*, hopefully capable of circling the globe.

Williams was extremely cautious at the controls of its first test flight. On later load test flights some of its fuel tanks were filled with 600 gallons of water as a safety measure in case of a crack-up. Boyd termed the *Uncle Sam* a bastard plane. Designed to carry a tremendous fuel load, it never lived up to expectations, and Levine's plans for a round-the-world flight soon were abandoned.

Then there was the mysterious fire! Levine's hangar was burned to the ground destroying the *Uncle Sam* and one other aircraft, a Triad. It was never learned how the blaze started. The insurance adjusters sifting through the charred ruins discovered that all instruments had been removed from both planes – a mystery unsolved. At that time Charlie Levine was in Europe with Mabel Boll. He had been suffering adverse publicity regarding worthless bonds used as security for a bank loan.

Regarding the ocean crossing attempt, Erroll Boyd initially had planned to take off from Old Orchard Beach, Maine, where Roger Q. Williams and Lewis Yancey's flight to Rome via Spain had originated the previous year. Boyd felt the beach would be ideal for a heavy take-off, similar to the hard, wet sands of Daytona Beach where Sir Malcolm Campbell was racing his *Bluebird* to new world speed records.

Several oil companies expressed interest in the proposed flight. Boyd accepted an offer from Tidewater Oil (Tydol) for $10,000 for using their product. This success prompted Boyd to engage a manager, Jack O'Brien, who operated a "speak-easy" on 35th Street in New York City. O'Brien's place was a hangout for aviators, one of the more famous being Bert Acosta who attracted many customers. O'Brien soon was instrumental in obtaining another $10,000 contract for Boyd from T.V. Rank, managing editor of Hearst Publications, for exclusive rights to the story of the pending flight.

Boyd then had a change of mind. Since Lindbergh had crossed from the U.S.A., he decided to start his flight from his native Canada.

The contract from the Tydol company was shelved with the hope of gaining a similar one in Canada. The contract with Hearst still held good.

When Levine's hangar had been destroyed by fire, Boyd was initially devastated thinking the *Columbia* had been destroyed in it. He learned from Sloan Taylor of the *Morning Telegraph* that Roger Williams had flown it a few days before the fire to St. Hubert Airport, Montreal, as well as one remaining Triad a few days later.

When and how Roger Q. Williams took them from the hangar without detection is unknown, and Williams never mentioned this episode in a book he wrote many years later. It is possible that Williams desired the *Columbia* for another record attempt himself.

In the interim, Erroll Boyd's personal bills were mounting. His father had helped him financially in the past but dreaded the idea of his flying the ocean and tried to stop the flight. Erroll, however, could not conceive of giving up his ambition at this stage. He never knew why Williams had moved the *Columbia* without informing him. It would appear that Charlie Levine again may have changed his mind in favour of Williams.

With flight manager O'Brien, Boyd travelled to Montreal by train to claim the *Columbia*. They checked into the Mount Royal Hotel, managed by the well-known Vernon Cardi who gave them a suite at the regular rate of $15 per day. They had hoped the hotel would donate it in exchange for the publicity received.

The next day Boyd and O'Brien located the two ships in the hangar at St. Hubert Airport and, armed with notarized papers from Sloan Taylor and Paul Jeans of the *Morning Telegraph*, took possession of the *Columbia*.

They then flew the trusty Bellanca to Toronto. Boyd's wife and children were staying at his father's summer home at Jackson's Point on Lake Simcoe, next door to the cottage of Col. T.H. Lennox, M.P. Flying overhead, Boyd dropped them a note scribbled on the back of an old weather map used in his record-breaking flight to Bermuda a month earlier – and his young daughter was the first to recover it.

Boyd had intended to originate the flight from Toronto but was unable to find financial backing there. Toronto then was a very conservative city in the early stages of the great depression. Before flying to Montreal a week later, however, the *Columbia* was rechristened the *Maple Leaf* in honour of Canada and the popular theme song of the day, *The Maple Leaf Forever*. It was also flown over large crowds at the Canadian National Exhibition.

When Boyd took off from Leaside Airport in Toronto for Montreal on September 1, 1930, he appeared to be very happy with the near-accomplishment of his fourteen-year dream. He showed newspaper reporters a picture of him with his youngest daughter, Virginia. The three-year-old later told them: "My dad is a good flier. He won't fall out of the plane."

Erroll Boyd's mother, his faithful booster, told the press that it had always been her son's ambition to fly the Atlantic, that he had an adventurous life, and that when he started to do anything he usually did it.

Upon their arrival at St. Hubert Airport, Montreal, the RCMP informed them that the *Columbia* had been grounded by Roger Williams, who claimed that Levine owed him a sum of money for back pay.

With bills already piling up, Boyd was faced with securing legal assistance to free the plane. This caused a further delay of several weeks, costing some ideal flying weather. He was also being bombarded with letters from Harry Connor asking to go along, emphasizing the lateness of the season to attempt the flight solo without a navigator. Boyd agreed with Connor but warned of the possibility of cancellation.

Harry Connor, navigator on the earlier flight to Bermuda, then flew up to Montreal with Bill Ulrich, later lost in an attempted flight to Rome in the *American Nurse*, the same plane in which Clyde Pangborn and Hugh Herndon flew around the world.

Connor and Ulrich brought with them one of the new artificial horizons by the Sperry company which was being loaned for the flight. This same instrument had been mounted originally in the famous Jimmy Doolittle's Lockheed Vega and tested by him at North Beach, now LaGuardia Airport. It had been balanced earlier by Elmer Sperry and was installed at St. Hubert airport by Vernon W. Silver of Canadian Wright, Ltd. To aid in calculating drift over the ocean the *Maple Leaf* had drift angle lines for every five to thirty degrees painted on the stabilizer on each side of the fin.

Boyd and O'Brien, lounging in their hotel room, were discussing how to release their aircraft from custody when Harry Connor turned up, decked out in a new tweed suit with cane, gloves, shiny shoes and bow-tie. Boyd and O'Brien were wearing creased clothes, and, rather than chance their credit, were reluctant to call the hotel valet for a pressing job.

"Harry, my boy," Boyd said, realizing Connor had not been too flush in New York, "you must have hit the jackpot! Where did you get that outfit?"

The grinning Connor explained he had visited the haberdashery in the hotel lobby, outfitted himself, and charged it to their room. How the charge escaped the credit manager's notice was a mystery.

In spite of tense relations with the hotel management, Boyd and O'Brien had made many friends in Montreal including the local manager of Canada Dry Ginger Ale who was to finance their fuel as far as Newfoundland.

A firm of lawyers headed by Thomas J. Coonan, K.C., came to the rescue of the grounded aircraft and offered to plead Boyd's case without fee. After some three weeks of court proceedings, Chief Justice Greenshields ruled in their favour and released the aircraft to Boyd's custody before its return to its rightful owner, Charles Levine, upon completion of the flight.

The days were getting shorter and time was crucial. Storms over the Atlantic were becoming more frequent with the change in seasons. Dr. James Kimball, the renowned New York meteorologist, was suggesting postponement until the following spring.

"We had no financial means to lay off for seven months, so the flight had to be now or never," Boyd said.

Their immediate problem was to leave the hotel without detection. But how? They had many friends among McGill University students, and a plan was plotted whereby O'Brien would stay in the suite as if nothing had happened. Erroll and Harry, with the help of a friendly waiter, would exit down the service elevator, through the kitchen and out into the alley. Outside the hotel they were met by the students who had already taken Harry's navigation instruments and books through the front lobby. The boys then drove them to their fraternity house near the campus where a party ensued with Boyd playing the piano while they sang and drank until the wee hours.

Early the next morning Boyd and Connor were driven to St. Hubert airport where the Bellanca was being fuelled for the leg to Harbour Grace, Newfoundland, courtesy of Canada Dry Ginger Ale, as a small crowd gathered around.

After the hangar dues were paid, Boyd and Connor had exactly $18 left. Fortunately, someone passed the hat to help them with their expenses, and even the local member of the RCMP contributed!

"You may well remember these were lean days," Boyd later wrote, "and the collection was a welcome gesture."

"All I had in mind at this time was to give the plane the gun and get as far away from Montreal as possible which at least would ensure us of a few days' respite from the law and the harassment of creditors," he said.

Boyd on seaplane float, Montreal, 1930 (Courtesy of Mrs. Fenn)

16

The Great Adventure Begins

THE TRANSATLANTIC adventure was underway on Saturday, September 13. They took off from St. Hubert airport, Montreal, in drizzling rain with poor visibility, their tanks loaded with 300 gallons of fuel. Harbour Grace in Newfoundland was some 900 miles to the east, and Boyd realized a landing at its unlighted airport after sundown would be inadvisable.

Halfway across Cape Breton Island, with winds still unfavourable, they realized they would not make Harbour Grace before dark. They turned around and landed at 5:30 p.m. at Charlottetown, Prince Edward Island, in a small farmer's field at Tea Hill just outside the city.

A small crowd turned up after the landing including Colonel J.S. Jenkins and the Lieutenant-Governor of the province. After tying down the ship, they were taken to Government House to register. Colonel Jack Jenkins, local chief physician, and his beautiful wife, Louise, became their chief benefactors, inviting them to stay at their home, Upton Farms, where a welcoming party lasted into the wee hours of the morning.

Adverse weather over Newfoundland and the North Atlantic delayed them there day by day for nine days. They were alarmed to learn that their flight manager, Jack O'Brien, was being held by the police in Montreal for non-payment of the hotel bill, but later learned a friend of his in the brewing business had helped him out financially.

During their stay in Prince Edward Island a haberdashery in Charlottetown presented Erroll with a new outfit so that he was no

Boyd and Connor with Jenkins family, Prince Edward Island, 1930
(Courtesy of the late Ken Molson)

longer shabbier than his navigator with his new suit so deftly acquired in Montreal.

The *Charlottetown Guardian* headlined their arrival: "Noted Airmen Believe In Safety First – TRANS-ATLANTIC FLIERS LAND HERE ON WAY TO NEWFOUNDLAND." In the story Boyd paid tribute to the new artificial horizon used flying blind over the mountains; to the navigation skills of Lieutenant Connor, and to Mr. Arthur Suddes of the Canadian Wright company at Montreal for the perfect functioning of their engine.

Pioneer flights in this era received extensive publicity. The same front page carried a photograph of U.S. president Herbert Hoover congratulating Diedenne Costes, who, with Maurice Bellonte, had just completed the first successful Paris to New York nonstop flight – a reverse of Lindbergh's track but tougher because of prevailing westerly winds.

The visit of Erroll Boyd and Harry Connor in 1930 to Prince Edward Island inspired the Jenkins family and spurred the development of aviation in Canada's eastern provinces.

Following their successful arrival in England, Erroll's wife in Toronto received the following telegram from Col. Jenkins on October 11:

Mrs. Jenkins and I are overjoyed with Erroll's success. Never has it been our privilege and honour to entertain a more distinguished, gallant and lovable a man. We share your happiness.

Dr. Jenkins had served in the First World War where he met a beautiful young lady from an affluent Pittsburgh family. When Louise and Jack were married in London on Armistice Day in 1918, their best man was Lord Beaverbrook (Max Aitken), formerly of New Brunswick, who would later serve with distinction as Winston Churchill's minister for aircraft production in World War II.

Shortly after the Boyd-Connor visit Dr. Jenkins built Upton Airport on his farm just north of the city. Licensed in January 1932, it was leased to Canadian Airways until 1938. As Upton was unsuitable for expansion, the present Charlottetown Airport was built a few miles away and soon became an important base for the British Commonwealth Air Training Plan in World War II.

Another important event happened after the Boyd visit. With her cosmopolitan background, Louise Jenkins found the quiet life of Prince Edward Island a little boring. Undoubtedly spurred by the Boyd-Connor visit, she became the first licensed woman pilot in Prince Edward Island in 1932. She achieved some notable flights in her own red and silver Puss Moth.

Two of Louise's daughters, Jessica and Joan, were aged ten and nine in the summer of 1930 and, many years later, remembered the exciting visit of Boyd and Connor. Jessica recalled often riding her pony to the early airport hoping someone would take her up for a flight. She reminisced about her mother's flying instructor, Gath K. Edward: "He was quite young at the time, probably in his early twenties, and I was madly in love with him. He taught me to dance." Gath Edward became a supervisory pilot with Trans-Canada Air Lines and was responsible later for the hiring of all Air Canada pilots.

Joan recalled that their two guests were always supposed to depart "the next day." Her mother, Louise, an early health advocate, had her prepare sandwiches of peanut butter, bacon and whole wheat bread each evening for the flyers to take with them. Louise, an avid horsewoman, had become a vegetarian after a visit to a meat packing plant.

Prince Edward Island's first woman pilot was a strong-willed,

Connor and Boyd in Harbour Grace, 1930 (Courtesy of Lamont M. Parsons)

Aircraft poised on runway, Harbour Grace, 1930 (Courtesy of Lamont M. Parsons)

charming woman. She wanted her aircraft to be registered CF-PEI to promote her home province, but the bureaucrats did not agree. Not one to accept no, she finally had Lord Beaverbrook's friend, Prime Minister R.B. Bennett, approve the designation.

More than four decades later a family friend, the late Reverend John McGillivray, a member of the Canadian Owners and Pilots Association (COPA), flew the reconstructed plane with Louise Jenkins as passenger to Ottawa for display in Canada's National Aviation Museum.

Many years later Boyd wrote that Connor and he had entertained the idea of staying over until 1931, the advice of the weather experts. He added light-heartedly: "After several days of revelling in this hospitality, Harry ran afoul of one of the town's social debutantes, so I decided it would be wise to make a quick departure."

Another interesting occurrence while Boyd and Connor were in Prince Edward Island was a report in the *New York Times* of September 18 that Roger Q. Williams had received a cable from Paris from Charles Levine that he had cancelled the projected transatlantic flight of his Bellanca. When informed of this press report Boyd questioned its authenticity and remarked, "I don't think we need worry about it."

The two airmen finally departed for Newfoundland on September 23. The airfield was extended 500 feet by the removal of a fence, the extra distance badly needed to ensure a safe take-off. Boyd said: "We were airborne without difficulty heading for Harbour Grace, some 500 miles away, with Harry subconsciously listening to the plaintive call of his paramour below!"

After four hours and twenty minutes Boyd made a smooth landing at their Atlantic departure point. The *Columbia* had been there before in 1928 with socialite entertainer Mabel Boll who aspired to be the first woman across the Atlantic in an airplane. She and her crew abandoned the crossing upon hearing that Amelia Earhart had landed in Wales from Trepassey Bay in a Fokker tri-motor on floats piloted by Wilmer Stultz.

Once in Harbour Grace Boyd and Connor suffered more than two weeks in weather delays. The airport log book there in the Conception Bay Museum records the following comments written by Harry Connor:

Weather conditions were favorable between P.E.I. and

Heritage site and Harbour Grace airport (Courtesy of William Oke)

Harbour Grace on Sept. 23rd, so we took off and had a wonderful trip here. We flew direct compass courses and made the passage in 4 hrs. 25 mins. averaging 111 mph We are now waiting favorable weather on the N. Atlantic for our flight to Croydon Airport, London, Eng. and are being well taken care of here. Everyone is cooperating with us, and we sincerely hope that it will not be long before Harbour Grace will be a terminal for regular transatlantic air service, and that the men who have worked so unselfishly for an airport here will reap their reward. We consider the runway here in good shape for a take-off with a heavy load and in an advantageous location.

Erroll and I had ample opportunity to check our ship and teamwork together on our recent N.Y. to Bermuda and return non-stop flight June 29, 1930, in the Columbia. We are well equipped for our flight. The motor, the original Wright J5 220 H.P. which Chamberlain and Levine flew to Germany with, and our instruments, are perfect. This flight is being undertaken by ourselves, and is the result of years of work and scientific experimenting. We hope to prove the accuracy of our methods, similarly as on our Bermuda flight. We believe in safety first, and if the flight is not a success, it will be our own fault! The Columbia is our baby!!!

The museum also contains a brass pistol that Boyd and Connor borrowed from airport commissioner, E.L. Oke. They had it engraved in England and returned to him. The inscription reads: "This very pistol was loaned to us by E.L. Oke of Harbour Grace and was carried on the first Canadian flight from Canada to England, October, 1930 in the airplane *Columbia* by Captain Boyd and Lieutenant Connor."

During their lengthy stay in Harbour Grace awaiting more favourable weather reports, the crew stayed at the Cochrane Hotel operated by Rose Archibald, whose two brothers owned the airstrip.

While they still had some of the $300 donation made by the city of Charlottetown, Boyd realized they would need additional funds to cover fuel and hotel expenses. Boyd, who had been sworn in at the post office to carry official mail, had been presented with two blocks of four stamps, presumably one for him and one for Connor. Boyd offered his block of four to the Archibalds in payment for $180 due. He learned later that this block of four was purchased two weeks later by Edson Fifield of the Scott Stamp & Coin Company for $1,800. Connor kept his stamps only to be relieved of them later by their former manager, O'Brien.

During their stay in Newfoundland, Boyd spent much time in the telegraph office checking weather reports. There he picked up a telegram for Connor from Frank Tichner, editor of *Aero Digest* with whom Boyd had tangled in 1929 over the accident rate of Coastal Airways. It read: "If you attempt this foolish flight with Boyd you will probably end up swimming across the ocean. Glad to send some money to pay your way back to New York. Last call." Connor would have nothing to do with Tichner's suggestion.

Harry Connor was an orphan with no close relations; his parents were killed in a train wreck when he was a small boy. He was referred to in those days as a "kiwi," one connected to aviation but unable to fly, but Boyd felt he was the best navigator at that time.

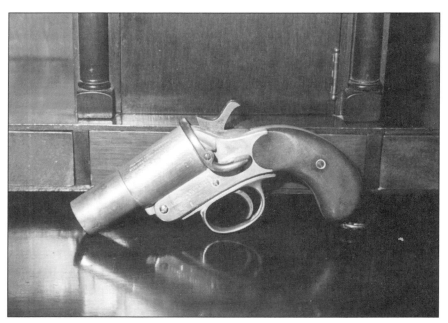

Flight's Very pistol in Harbour Grace Museum (Courtesy of William Oke)

During the night of October 8 before the take-off Boyd and Connor got little sleep. Boyd thought about his home, his family and the hazards of the flight. Connor also must have had some concern on his mind also, but they never spoke of it to each other. They obviously recalled the many previous air crews lost at sea without mentioning them.

Block of four stamps carried, value $20,000 in 1995

17

Previous Failed Canadian Attempts

A PAUSE to review earlier efforts by Canadians to fly across the Atlantic Ocean will magnify the difficulties facing Erroll Boyd in his ambition to be the first Canadian across. The successful New York-Paris flight of Charles Lindbergh in *Spirit of St. Louis* in May of 1927 generated new interest and investment in aviation and resulted in many attempts at new distant flights – and many failures.

Among the motivations for crossing the Atlantic Ocean – fame, fortune, and linking distant communities – was a simple one: that it simply existed. Its watery vastness and its unpredictable weather challenged the adventurer.

This enthusiasm or Atlantic fever spread to Canada, a country relatively small in population yet which had supplied a record number of wartime fliers, including four of the top ten aces in World War I – Billy Bishop, Raymond Collishaw, Billy Barker and Don McLaren. The latter became the first employee of Trans-Canada Air Lines (now Air Canada) in 1937, after serving with James Richardson's Canadian Airways as pilot and regional manager.

The Carling Brewery of London, Ontario, offered a $25,000 prize for any Canadian or British pilot who could make the 3,900 mile nonstop flight from London, Ontario, to London, England. Great publicity for any company, the project nevertheless was a genuine effort to meet the demands of many of Canada's war veterans.

Hundreds applied but lacked the necessary experience, equipment and financing.

The Carling company quickly realized the need to change the rules so it engaged experts to purchase the best plane and equipment available. This technical committee included Commodore F.G. Ericson, Swedish by birth but well known in U.S. and Canadian aviation circles in World War I. As no suitable Canadian plane or motor was available and British firms were unable to supply one for a year, an American Stinson monoplane with a Wright Whirlwind motor was selected. The plane was named *Sir John Carling* in honour of the prominent London citizen and founder of the brewery.

After some thirty applicants were interviewed, Captain Terrence Tully and Lieutenant James Medcalf were selected as the crew for the flight. The City of London's engineering department prepared a long runway for the takeoff just east of the city. As an added safety measure, it was decided that a stop at Newfoundland for refuelling would be permitted.

Canada's first air mail stamp at twenty-five cents was issued by the Canadian postal authorities for this London to London flight. It included a picture of the two airmen and their aircraft. Due to weight limitations imposed by the flight's organizer, only forty-two prepaid items were carried with the bag and contents being just over two pounds.

For some unknown reason one stamped flight cover was not carried on the *Sir John Carling*. The Canadian Aerophilatelic Society reported that it was sold at an auction in early 1995 for $40,000 U.S.!

The flight initially took off from London, Ontario, on the early morning of August 29, 1927, with some 10,000 spectators on hand. The weather deteriorated to a ceiling of 200 feet by the time they reached Kingston, Ontario, and, with mountains and obstructions ahead, they returned to London. When conditions improved, they left again on September 1 but adverse weather forced them to land at Caribou, Maine. On September 5 they finally arrived at Harbour Grace.

At this same time two other flights were preparing for an eastbound transoceanic crossing. One was a Windsor, Ontario, to Windsor, England, flight to be flown by Canadian bush pilot C.A. "Duke" Schiller, accompanied by American sportsman Phil S. Wood, a brother of renowned boat racer, Gar Wood. The other, the *Old Glory*, sponsored by the Hearst Newspapers, was planning to take off from Portland, Maine.

The *Sir John Carling* narrowly avoided disaster at Harbour Grace when spilled gas was ignited. A group of bystanders helped push the plane out of danger. During their stopover at the Cochrane House, where Boyd and Connor would later stay, Tully and Medcalf received word that *Old Glory* out of Maine was reported overdue and presumed missing at sea. That did not deter them.

On the morning of September 7 many spectators at Harbour Grace witnessed the take-off and watched the flight speed eastward over Conception Bay until it faded from view. They were the last to ever see the *Sir John Carling*.

The *S.S. Kyle* in Harbour Grace was chartered to search and a few days later picked up some bits of wreckage from *Old Glory* but no trace of the *Sir John Carling* has ever been found. Within one week three planes had met disaster attempting to fly the Atlantic. The other was a westbound attempt in the *Saint Raphael* from Britain carrying its financial backer, Princess Lowenstein-Wertheim and pilots L.P. Hamilton and F.F. Minchin. They vanished without a trace.

Only a few hours after the *Sir John Carling's* takeoff from Harbour Grace, Schiller and Wood arrived there for their transatlantic attempt. The American citizen Phil Wood had earlier been refused entry in the London-to-London flight, so he made plans for a rival flight. He purchased a similar Stinson monoplane in Michigan and engaged Schiller, an experienced pilot with the Ontario Provincial Air Service, to fly it from Windsor, Ontario, to the vicinity of the Windsor Castle in England. The plane was named the *Royal Windsor* and a friendly rivalry sprang up between the two Canadian cities of London and Windsor.

Schiller and Wood could not take off immediately until a small leak in one of their tanks had been repaired. While staying at the Cochrane House they learned that the *Sir John Carling* was overdue and probably lost at sea. Friends prevailed upon them to give up the attempt.

Due to the high fatality rate over the North Atlantic that year, Prime Minister Mackenzie King was threatening to introduce legislation prohibiting such flights from Canada. The Windsor mayor and organizing committee and British authorities also advocated cancellation of the flight. Schiller and Wood flew hundreds of miles out to sea looking for their lost friends but finally returned to Windsor.

Regarding the loss of the *Sir John Carling* at sea, the Canadian representatives of Lloyd's of London had assumed $10,000 risk on both Tully and Medcalf by verbal arrangement. They paid up after deduction of the unpaid premium. The $25,000 prize money was added to a trust fund for the benefit of the two widows and three children of the airmen.

Weather reports from ships at sea around this time indicated the likelihood that both the *Sir John Carling* and *Old Glory* had encountered violent weather including possible thunderstorms. Their unsuccessful attempts to fly across took place outside the peak of the summer season with its more favourable weather and longer daylight hours.

18

Atlantic Crossing

THE DEPARTURE airport at Harbour Grace, Newfoundland, holds a prominent spot in aviation history. Out of twenty transoceanic flights attempted from Harbour Grace in the 1927-1936 period, eleven were successful, four were unaccounted for, two crashed on take-off, two aborted their flights for various reasons, and one crash-landed off the coast of Ireland with the pilot being rescued. Charles Kingsford-Smith, Wiley Post, Amelia Earhart and James Mollison were some of the fliers using Harbour Grace in this 1927-1936 period.

The safety rate for flights from Harbour Grace was better than from many other departure points. In this adventurous era of the late 1920s and early 1930s, many airmen and women were lost at sea. Not only were their aircraft, engines and instruments crude by present standards, but the crews lacked formal training in instrument flying. The probable cause of many disappearances at sea was loss of control at night in turbulent conditions causing a deadly spiral dive with possible structural failure.

The official air mail on the Boyd flight, consisting of some 300 letters, was the first to be carried from Canada (Newfoundland) to Europe. Its potential value to collectors was so great that even forged overprints were produced. Shortly after the flight, a man purporting to be a film company representative turned up in St. John's seeking stamps for a transatlantic flight movie. Since all had been sold out, he persuaded a local printer to copy the surcharge on blocks of four and sold them to an unsuspecting stamp dealer in the U.S.

"For many years I've waited for this opportunity," Boyd had said. "I've set my heart on it. The Bermuda flight has been accomplished . . .

as far as worrying goes – none for me because I am navigated by an old partner who knows his Atlantic. If we know our Bermuda onions, why not our north Atlantic icicles?"

The flight plan required flying east true from St. John's to thirty-five degrees west longitude, and then the great circle route to Swansea, Bristol and Croydon. An hour and thirty-five minutes after their 16:20Z take-off, they were sighted and reported by the freighter *Quaker City* "flying due eastward only 200 feet above the water at a point approximately 100 miles east-northeast of Cape Race, the eastern tip of Newfoundland."

The afternoon weather remained good, but Connor's observations showed them to be making only sixty-eight mph ground speed with an air speed of ninety-three. By sunset, their ground speed had increased only to seventy mph while maintaining "a low altitude of between 600 and 1,000 ft. in order to take advantage of a better 'pull' and less head wind."

Using the planet Venus and the stars, Connor was able to check their position at frequent intervals during the early part of the flight although he reported "the old ship, still with a heavy load, vibrated when I climbed back of the main tank to take observations." The observation hatch was fitted with a removable windshield to permit taking of observations all around the horizon. The windshield made it possible to hold a sextant steady against the slip stream.

The vibration during the take-off from Harbour Grace had made the earth inductor compass dial unserviceable making it necessary to rely on the two magnetic compasses. Connor praised Boyd who had ample practice on the earlier Bermuda flight of steering an accurate course to the nearest degree.

After one and one-half hours of night flying, battery failure required the use of the emergency flashlight to energize the phosphorous material on the flight instruments. Later, in London, Boyd said: "Boy, it was dark! I felt as though I was piloting a car in a coal mine."

At about 22:40Z the fliers passed over the Cunard ship *Lancastria* and signalled her by flashlight spelling out the name *Columbia* in Morse code. Approximately 440 miles from St. John's, their average ground speed was only seventy-two mph. The easterly winds gradually decreased and backed to northward. Approaching longitude forty degrees, they encountered cumulus and cumulo-nimbus clouds and started climbing up through the clouds from 5,000 feet.

The Sperry artificial horizon proved to be an invaluable aid in the night and blind flying, recording the plane's actual attitude relative to the horizon. This instrument, on its first Atlantic flight, had been installed by Canadian Wright at St. Hubert airport.

After encountering rain, the crew were unable to check their position or drift. A short time later, they flew into some very rough air which indicated that the wind had freshened. By dead reckoning navigation, they calculated by 03:30Z that they had reached thirty-five degrees west longitude. They then changed their course northwards as planned to allow them to follow the great circle steamer track.

While climbing through the clouds, they saw their outside thermometer drop to the freezing level. Boyd had painted a black strip on the leading edge of the wing, a trick he had learned in the 1920s. With the aid of a flashlight, he could see white particles of ice forming on this strip. Immediately he descended on a southerly heading which he held for a considerable time. Reaching an area of warmer temperature, he climbed back into the clouds on an east-northeasterly course calculated by dead reckoning.

They finally came out at 12,000 ft. Boyd later said, "Believe me, that was the best moon I ever saw!". They were tossed around considerably, and tremendous mountains of clouds extended upward above this level. The weather continued to be extremely rough throughout the remainder of the night. They estimated they were making a ground speed of 138 to 140 mph although the air speed registered only ninety to ninety-two mph.

Any accurate observations were impossible under these weather conditions, and it was necessary to weave in between the cloud mountains for the remainder of the night. Since Connor was not a pilot, Boyd had to do all of the flying. Whenever Boyd felt sleepy, Connor held a wet sponge soaked in ice water to the back of his neck.

Boyd earlier had felt the strain of having had practically no sleep the night before, and was continually drinking black coffee and taking aspirins. He later wrote:

> We had a quart silver flask of brandy which had been
> given to us for the flight by Col. Jenkins. It went
> untouched as I knew it would be fatal to even take a jigger

– as deadly as a dozen sleeping pills, or like a shipwrecked sailor drinking salt water. Nevertheless, I would have liked a swig!

The food and refreshment carried included chocolate, chicken sandwiches and ginger ale.

Glad to see dawn after a long ten and one-half hours of darkness, they observed three layers of clouds. Descending to 500 feet of altitude they found a thirty-five mph tailwind. But it was too rough at that altitude so they climbed back to 8,000 feet. After an hour they were able to fly safely at an altitude of 1,500 feet.

Due to the great refraction in the early morning, the navigator was unable to take a reliable observation by position lines of the sun until 09:40Z. This new position at forty-seven degrees north, eighteen degrees west put them 113 statute miles south of the steamer track. On the course being steered, they were heading for the Bay of Biscay, and it was necessary to change some twenty-five degrees to the left towards Land's End and London.

Because of aircraft noise, communication between pilot and navigator was normally by note. When Connor was shooting the sun from the opening in the top of the aeroplane at the rear of the main gas tank, he would jerk a piece of string tied to the pilot's wrist. One jerk was to change course ninety degrees to the right. The second jerk of the string was to reverse direction 180 degrees. This enabled Connor to get an accurate shot from two directions, the method used so successfully on the earlier Bermuda flight.

Boyd and Connor made the disconcerting discovery that, due to a clogged line, the 100 gallons of fuel from the main reserve tank would not pump up into the gravity tank in the right wing. They tried to rectify the problem but finally admitted defeat. It was later determined that a chemical reaction had left a deposit sealing off this fuel flow.

After pondering the risks of ditching near a passing ship whose sailors would pick them up if they didn't sink, they made a decision that they probably could make landfall. Still about 560 statute miles from Land's End, Boyd throttled back to reduce fuel consumption from twelve gallons per hour to about eight. With a greatly reduced air speed, they decided to rely on very strong southwesterly winds south of the low pressure area over Ireland and the British Isles.

Approaching the coast, they spotted numerous vessels, with the Scilly Isles soon appearing on their port bow. They arrived over the Scilly Isles at 16:02Z, almost a full day after departure. The navigator was making for Plymouth, England, because he did not think Boyd could make a good landing on the islands. But Erroll advised him that he could land safely and that he did not want to risk the last twenty-three miles of water between the Isles and Land's End.

As a precaution against fire, the dump valve was opened, releasing the 100 gallons of unusable fuel from the reserve tank into the ocean. Connor stayed in the very back of the cabin to allow for a better centre of gravity during the landing. Although it was high tide, Boyd set the *Maple Leaf* down on the sloping beach between two streams at Tresco, Scilly Islands, stopping within a few inches of the water's edge and only 200 feet from where the landing gear first touched the soft sand. The fuel tanks were almost empty!

"This beach was the narrowest landing place I had ever attempted," Boyd said. "The tide was full and we had less than fifty yards between the water and the rocks."

Navigator Harry Connor commented: "I didn't think any human being could land a ship on that narrow strip of beach."

Tresco, second largest of the Scilly Isles, is only two miles long by three-quarters of a mile wide.

"There were moments when Connor and I wondered whether we would ever again have the privilege of shaking hands with anybody in this world," Boyd said. "But we cheated death and defeated the Atlantic and today are thanking fortune that we are alive."

19

Overseas at Last

AFTER EMERGING from the cockpit on the beach at Tresco, Boyd
reported that he and Connor staggered around like a couple of
drunken sailors until they regained full use of their legs. They had
been in cramped positions for over twenty-four hours and both were
nearly deaf from the continuous roar of the motor.

Boyd's first thoughts were to get the aircraft onto higher ground
where she would be safe from the incoming tide and salt spray.
Fortunately a small horse and buggy came along with a coil of rope
which was attached to the tail-skid. With this old method of
horsepower the ship was pulled onto one of the higher dunes and
made fast for the night.

Then Erroll inquired about the nearest pub where he downed a
couple of brandy and sodas while Harry quenched his thirst with ale
as the news of their arrival spread rapidly. Soon they were hosted by
the islands' governor, Major D. Smith and his daughter, in a beautiful
castle which had been occupied on occasions by the late King Edward
VII.

The two guests were feasted at a dinner of wild pheasant and
hare. Partway through the sumptuous meal, Erroll was having
difficulty staying awake and was excused. He sank into an old-
fashioned four-poster feather bed with heated bags of salt between the
sheets to provide warmth.

About four hours later Boyd was awakened by an excited Harry
Connor. Dozens of cables were being received on the island. Many
were offers of contracts for exclusive stories which they could not
accept because of their previous commitment to Hearst. The

governor had already requested the air force to fly in fifty gallons of high octane gas for them.

"What a change!" Erroll said. "Thirty hours ago we were broke and had to dispose of precious stamps to pay for the airport bill in Newfoundland."

The next morning they had ample time to explore the castle and prepare the aircraft for its last leg to London's airport at Croydon. Nearly every man, woman and child on the island seemed to be helping to prepare a makeshift runway of boards on the sand. The ship had been refuelled with the gas flown in by flying boat from Plymouth.

Would they be able to take off successfully on this improvised runway while the tide was out? Fortunately the wind was blowing twenty mph and the lightly loaded ship was in the air in less than 100 yards. As they neared London, Boyd recalled the area well from his

Aircraft on beach in Scilly Isles, 10 October 1930 (Courtesy of the late Ken Molson)

flying days in the RNAS some fifteen years ago. The reduced visibility around the big city also reminded him of his flights into the smog of Pittsburgh.

They landed at London after a flight of less than three hours from the Scilly Isles. For Erroll Boyd it was the completion of a long-cherished dream. For the record, it was the only west-to-east crossing by air in 1930, and carried the first official air mail on the route.

Among the crowd greeting them at Croydon was the controversial Charlie Levine, the first to reach the ship as they were taxiing in. He jumped up and clung to the left wing strut and asked Boyd, "How was the trip?"

"Only fair," Boyd replied.

Levine was obviously very happy to see his plane safe and sound on British soil, no doubt remembering when he landed there with difficulty on his first spectacular solo flight from Paris in 1927. Also among the crowd at the airport was RNAS veteran E.A. Priest who had served with Boyd at Dunkirk in the Great War.

It took nearly half an hour for Boyd and Connor to get out of the plane as the cameras clicked and the crowd refused to move.

Captain Boyd soon was linked by phone to all of his excited family in Toronto. They anxiously had followed the many reports of the *Maple Leaf*'s progress, some of which originated from ships at sea. His parents, wife and four daughters were thrilled with the news of the safe arrival.

When Erroll talked to his oldest daughter, Bey, age twelve, she said all the family were well except six-year-old Honor who became ill while eating four bananas celebrating her dad's safe arrival.

His father said that Col. Billie Bishop, Canada's famous wartime flier, had telephoned his compliments the previous night. What he did not tell his son was that the famous ace did not have the heart to call earlier because of his pessimism about Boyd's chances of getting through that late in the year!

His mother recalled to reporters that overcoming obstacles had always been her son's specialty from a very young age. A mother's faith in her son helps him to do greater things, she said. His more conservative father, who had initially opposed the flight, was very pleased.

Their reception in England was subdued slightly by the tragic crash a few days previously of the airship R-101 in France with heavy loss of life including many VIPs. Flags were still being flown at half-mast.

A few days later Captain Boyd and Lieut. Connor flew the *Maple Leaf* from Croydon to Cardington, circled the graves of the R-101 victims, and dropped a wreath bearing the inscription, "From airmen to airmen."

Mobbed by the press on their arrival, Boyd was warned by Mr. Ritchie of Hearst not to jeopardize their $10,000 contract for the exclusive story. After speaking to his family by telephone, Boyd and his navigator were rushed to the Savoy Hotel where they were interviewed for a lengthy cable to the Hearst publications.

In it they stressed the experimental nature of their trip to advance the science of aviation and transoceanic flying. While believing their plane was capable of a round trip, they mentioned the dangers with one engine, but stated they would not hesitate with a suitable multi-motored aircraft.

Among the many formal congratulations, Sir Richard Squires, premier of Newfoundland, stated with pride that Harbour Grace, famous departure point for Atlantic flights, was his birthplace. War hero Colonel Billy Bishop V.C. praised Boyd's keen judgement in not carrying wireless equipment which might have prevented him from reaching land. Sir George Perley, acting Canadian Prime Minister in Ottawa, had helped Boyd get his transfer from the Army and commission in the Royal Naval Air Service some fifteen years earlier in World War I when Perley was High Commissioner for Canada in London.

This transatlantic flight by a Canadian pilot, much of it conducted at night and in instrument conditions, proved that Erroll Boyd was one of the few experienced instrument pilots of his era. The weather conditions and available daylight during turbulent October differed greatly from that of May and June.

In London, Boyd and Connor were kept busy answering telegrams and writing testimonials for manufacturers of various products carried on the flight, important ones being the new Sperry artificial horizon, AC mica-sparkplugs and Shell petroleum who ran a large ad, "BOYD Conquers Atlantic on SHELL."

Industry officials were astounded at the use of an old Hartzell wooden propeller that Boyd had purchased for $12 from a student pilot near Wilmington, Delaware. It had been stored in a hayloft on a farm. In later years it was on display in the meeting place of the Quiet Birdmen in New York. The aircraft earlier had been equipped with a hollow metal propeller but some of these had been flying to pieces under stress.

Among the officials greeting the two airmen was the Prime Minister of Canada, R.B. Bennett, who was in London for the Imperial Conference. The two airmen had breakfast with Bennett and Premier G.T. Ferguson of Ontario at the Mayflower Hotel. Boyd learned that they had been in touch with his father in Toronto who had asked them to try to dissuade Boyd and Connor from their plans to fly home. Many years later Boyd wrote:

> I think both of us have regretted allowing ourselves to be talked out of our intent. Checking over our flight from Harbour Grace, I didn't think we could have encountered any worse weather. Although there probably would have been headwinds to contend with, we would have taken off on a course from Baldonnel, Ireland, shortening our span of ocean flying by some 400 miles.

19

Being Wined and Dined

INVITATIONS were pouring into Boyd and Connors' London headquarters at the Savoy for luncheons, dinners and night club parties all over town. One came from the U.S. ambassador, Charles Dawes, who eventually told them they would be "a couple of damn fools to attempt a return flight" and to rest on their laurels. Boyd assumed that the Canadian politicians had been in touch with him, but the advice was accepted.

On their tour of London they were showered with gifts including the very best from Bond Street tailors. They met Tallulla Bankhead, the rage of the London stage. Beatrice Lillie gave them a party at her home. Among the many guests was the former Prince of Wales, later Duke of Windsor.

One highlight at the party was when Harry Connor was greeted by Tallulla. Her embrace literally lifted him off the floor, leading one English peer to comment to Erroll, "Many a chap would have given a thousand quid to have the same experience with Tallulla."

One evening a London newspaper columnist had dinner with Boyd and Connor and Colonel Moore-Brabazon, the first Englishman to fly an airplane. The next day Moore-Brabazon was appointed to the commission of inquiry investigating the R-101 airship disaster.

The columnist, fascinated to study at close quarters the two men who had just flown the Atlantic, wrote about:

> The Canadian, Captain Boyd, thirty-nine years old,
> stout and good-natured, but a romantic, and the

American, Lieutenant Connor, a scientific fanatic in regard to all forms of navigation.

To Lieutenant Connor the Atlantic crossing means simply a test for his instruments—and nothing more. And death would imply nothing but a failure of those instruments.

Here, nevertheless, as in other walks of life, the materialist is dominated by the romantic. It is Captain Boyd who provides the driving force of the partnership.

After dinner the four drank toasts, first to their host, Moore-Brabazon, in recognition of his pioneering position in aviation. He was toasted as "the old cabhorse." They then toasted the two "forgotten airmen" whose wonderful feat had received so little recognition from the official aeronautical bodies.

While in London Erroll Boyd apparently was in the process of acquiring the ownership of the Bellanca *Columbia*. While renamed the *Maple Leaf* by Boyd, it is better known by its original name with which it earlier had established many endurance, load and efficiency records.

Shortly after Erroll's arrival in London, his brother Norman had received a vague cable from him enquiring if the city of Toronto would be interested in buying the aircraft "worth five times as much as asked." With so many unemployed at the time, the local politicians were divided over the issue but had insufficient information to make a decision. This cable may have been initiated at the suggestion of then-owner Charlie Levine.

When Sherwin Cottingham, a wealthy Canadian living in England, heard the aircraft was for sale, he immediately offered to buy the *Columbia* for the airmen as a token of admiration for their flight.

"I have never known a more generous action than that of Mr. Cottingham," said Captain Boyd. "Canadians the world over will appreciate it deeply."

The following is from Boyd's notes made probably in the late 1950s: "It seems strange, but if you knew Charlie, that he sold the famous *Columbia* to Sherwin Cottingham for a mere $15,000 when only three years before he refused an offer from Mayor Jimmy Walker of New York City to part with the plane for $100,000. Another of his many idiosyncrasies."

The *London Daily Express* editorialized on this appropriate gift, but asked why officialdom or their usually enterprising flying clubs had not seized on this splendid achievement and publicly proclaimed its authors.

Cottingham, a paint manufacturer and aviation enthusiast linked to both Montreal and England, then donated the aircraft to his friend, Erroll Boyd. Possibly that explains the following events described under the press caption, "Why the Vicar's daughter flew."

On the night of October 30, 1930, Erroll Boyd and Harry Connor had packed their bags for a flight to continental Europe early the next morning. Late that evening Erroll received a phone call from a Maisie Procter who said she was at the Kit Kat Club with Sherwin Cottingham who had suggested she go along on the flight to Berlin.

Boyd asked Maisie to have Sherwin telephone back in about twenty minutes to verify the request. Boyd meanwhile was contemplating his wife's reaction and possible adverse publicity in hometown newspapers.

Cottingham called back explaining that Maisie was taking flying lessons from a school he operated at Croydon, and since the *Columbia* had dual controls, could Boyd give her some instruction enroute? After consultation with Connor, Boyd concurred and agreed to meet her at the Savoy at 5 a.m. He later learned she was an acquaintance of the Prince of Wales and daughter of the Vicar of St. Thomas, Ryde, Isle of Wight.

Boyd and Connor were asleep when Maisie telephoned back asking if she could bring along a friend, Vivian Stayner (daughter of Lieutenant Colonel Stayner of Ryde). The main fuel tank had already been removed and replaced with two seats making ample room so they agreed. Next morning, following a flight over the area where Boyd had been shot down in World War I, the party of four landed at Amsterdam to be greeted by an official reception committee headed by the mayor.

While Boyd knew some Dutch, he was always embarrassed at his limitations in speaking foreign languages. From the airport they joined a motorcade which took them to The Hague's famous Central Hotel where Boyd spent time during internment in 1916. After many welcome receptions, they visited the haunts of British officers interned during the war.

The next day they landed at Templehof in Berlin shortly after dark, and were greeted by their largest crowds and receptions ever.

Harry Connor claimed it exceeded any following his later round-the-world flight as navigator with Howard Hughes in 1938. Germany was impressed that America had produced the first aircraft to cross the Atlantic twice spanning the gap between continents in a matter of hours.

World heavyweight boxing champion Max Schmeling and his manager were involved in reception arrangements. Even a parade was organized honouring the airmen, who stayed in a suite previously occupied by the Kaiser at the luxurious Adlon Hotel, later destroyed by bombing in World War II. In the grim times of 1917 when the Kaiser's war had not been going well, famous airmen temporarily returned from the front were registered comfortably here: names such as Richthofen, Udet and Goering. Their comfortable rooms were paid for by a Dutchman named Tony Fokker who had made it his business to provide airplanes to the highest bidder, in this case the Imperial German Air Force.

Boyd and Connor took off for LeBourget airport, Paris, without Maisie and Vivian, tagged as the *Columbia* girls by the Berlin newspapers. Their parents in England had become concerned, and they were put on a plane for home. A subsequent press report indicated that one of them, Vivian Stayner, married a rubber planter a couple of months later at Marylebone, London, with her flying friend, Maisie Proctor, in attendance.

The reception in France was a little more reserved. Boyd and Connor attended a reception with the famous French fliers, Coste and Bellonte, who had chalked up a world east-to-west record from Paris to New York in *The Question Mark*.

That same evening in Paris, Boyd and Connor were guests of Clifford Harmon, the American who originated the Harmon Trophy award. According to Boyd's notes:

> I was officially presented with the Harmon Trophy
> for Canada for the Atlantic crossing, distinction which was
> never fully realized although authentic. Col. Chuck
> Kerrewood, an American pilot who was representing Mr.
> Harmon in the United States, had been designated to
> make the final presentation, but no one seemed to be able
> to locate the trophy. The last holder was a Canadian pilot
> by the name of Stevenson.

Captain Frederick J. Stevenson, World War I ace and renowned bush pilot, was killed at The Pas, Manitoba, on January 5, 1928, and Winnipeg's airport was named after him. The probable reason for the lack of follow-up on the presentation of the Harmon Trophy was a blistering attack on Harmon and his International League of Aviators by the crusty editor of *The Aeroplane*, C.G. Grey. Grey claimed that the flight was only a stunt, and that it was not a Canadian achievement as claimed, presumably because the navigator and the aircraft were American.

Boyd later received a letter dated November 12, 1930, from president Clifford Harmon stating that his board of directors unanimously had elected Erroll president of the Canadian section of the International League of Aviators.

Back in London Captain Erroll Boyd and Lieutenant Harry Connor talked about aviation for forty-five minutes on November 6 with the Prince of Wales in St. James Palace. Six years later the popular prince would abandon the monarchy to marry the American divorcee, Wally Simpson.

"The Prince has a sound knowledge of aviation in all its branches," said Boyd. "It is surprising for a man who has not made aviation his profession. We told him all about our flight and it was just as if we were talking to a fellow pilot. He asked me, for example, if it would be possible for him to fly from Montreal to his ranch in Alberta when he goes to Canada again."

21

Welcomed Back in Canada

MONTREAL opened her arms wide to welcome Captain Erroll Boyd and Lieutenant Harry Connor back in Canada as the Canadian Pacific liner, *Duchess of Bedford*, steamed into the harbour amid a babel of ship sirens and an escort of aircraft overhead in the sunny November sky.

Erroll remembered their hasty departure on a wet, rainy morning some two months previously when fewer than one hundred spectators at St. Hubert airport cheered them on their way, and a single, enterprising reporter flew just under the low overcast sky to photograph their departure.

Among the pilots flying overhead as the liner docked were J.C. Webster, Roy Foss and Marshall Foss of the Montreal Light Aeroplane Club and Captains Ayres and Troup flying more recent Bellanca models. In one plane was Elwood Hosmer who, two years earlier, had attempted to fly the Atlantic with Captain Frank Courtney in the flying boat *Whale*. They were forced down at sea and fortunately were picked up by a passing steamer after several days afloat. A Stearman of Canadian Airways also circled overhead to honour the returning heroes.

A host of cameras clicked as dignitaries boarded the ocean liner for the formal welcoming ceremonies. Mrs. Boyd, wearing an airplane-shaped diamond brooch, and her three-year-old daughter, Virginia, were also the centre of considerable attention, having boarded the *Duchess* earlier in the provincial capital at Quebec. Happiness radiated in the greetings extended by alderman Dr. Fred Gilday representing Mayor Camillien Houde, J.H. Rainville,

111

chairman of the harbour commission, and alderman Allan Bray, chairman of the city's executive committee whose words were carried by radio.

Salvo upon salvo of cheers punctuated their welcoming remarks but the volume was small in comparison with the ovations extended as they left the liner an hour and a half after its docking. The protecting group of police helped push the airmen through the throngs as Boyd sought section B and Connor section C to claim their baggage. No special provisions had been made for customs clearance and the inspectors insisted on doing their duty.

"Must I open my trunk?" Boyd asked in a plaintive voice.

"You have a new trunk," said the customs examiner. "All purchases abroad must be declared."

"I have a few blue suits and other things," Boyd declared.

"What value do you place on your new belongings?" came the next question.

"I don't know," replied Boyd who gave a rough guess.

"Well, I think I ought to get an appraiser. Wait here and I shall try to find one," the customs examiner stated while the crowd murmured, wondering what was coming next.

The suggestion was then made that Boyd might leave his belongings at the wharf until next day when he could return and have them appraised. The superintendent acquiesced and a larger crowd cheered them as they left the shed and entered a taxi to the Mount Royal Hotel from which they had departed so hastily in the past.

In the meantime their aircraft, the *Maple Leaf*, damaged in the loading at Liverpool, would be unloaded and sent to St. Hubert for repair and reassembly. Their manager, O'Brien, had made arrangements for their appearance as guests of the management of the Frolics in addition to a charitable appearance for the unemployed.

The press also reported that the owner of the aircraft, Sherwin Cottingham, a Montrealer now resident in London, was in the process of presenting the aircraft to the airmen in the interests of aviation.

The evening following their arrival in Montreal, Boyd and Connor were honoured at a civic banquet given by Mayor Houde in the Mount Royal Hotel. The mayor himself, who had personally supervised the arrangements, was unable to attend and alderman Gilday presided in his place. Judges, legislators, distinguished professional men and consul-generals were present to proclaim the success of the first transatlantic flight by a Canadian.

During the many tributes roars of cheering broke out followed by the singing of *Hail, the gang's all here* and *Il a gagné ses épaulettes.*

Captain Boyd spoke briefly and falteringly, but the guests were not so easily satisfied. Cries urging him to tell more about the flight finally brought him to his feet again. Boyd told them they had read it all in the press and then gracefully heaped praise on his navigator whom he hoped would stay a while in Canada.

"He asked me to go down to the States with him," Captain Boyd said, "but I told him he could have the Statue and I would keep the Liberty."

His second address ended quickly and no amount of persuasion would bring him to his feet again. Harry Connor then spoke even more briefly: "I am happy to have flown the Atlantic with the first Canadian."

Shouts persuaded him to rise a second time when he thanked everybody and alluded to Chief Justice Greenshields' dismissal of the court action that would have prevented their take-off.

Greenshields spoke next to welcome "our heroes" and declared the court action had dealt with an unjust claim to delay the flight. After his ruling he recalled saying to a colleague: "I am afraid I have sent two gallant gentlemen on an adventure from which they will never return," and then he expressed his joy in having them back.

"I wondered how they would have the courage to start off in such a small, light craft," Greenshields said, "and I asked one of them if he realized the risk.'Yes, we realize it,' he answered, 'But do you realize the risk you take in crossing Sherbrooke Street at five o'clock?'"

Another guest at the civic banquet was Thomas Coonan, K.C., who had provided free legal service to the fliers during the court action.

A.A. Gardiner of the CNR, in congratulating the airmen, referred to a recently announced merger of airways and railroads. Father Blanchard, representing the Archbishop of Montreal, spoke of spiritual flight after death and the fact that modern aviators had found a way to fly without dying first. Helen Kane of stage and screen fame paid her respect to the two aviators by singing a new song, *I'm takin' a chance with you.*

ONWARD HOME TO TORONTO

The following was captioned in the *Toronto Star* of November 25, 1930:

TORONTO OPENS ARMS TO GREET NATIVE SON AFTER OCEAN FLIGHT

Capt. Erroll Boyd Barely Misses Crash in Landing at Century Airport

SKILL SAVED HIM

The day before their departure for Toronto, Boyd test flew his aircraft from Montreal's St. Hubert airport with Arthur Suddes, manager of Canadian Wright. The capacious gasoline tanks used for transatlantic flights had been removed and chairs substituted so that Mrs. Boyd and her young daughter could travel in comfort.

The Boyd family were at the airport the next morning shortly after dawn, disappointed at the steady rain. In running up the engine, Boyd discovered a balky magneto and called for Suddes to make repairs while the fliers watched the dull sky for a break. A reception in Toronto had been planned for the early afternoon.

Impatient to get to Toronto, Boyd decided to start although visibility and ceiling were poor. After helping his wife and daughter to board, he took off at 10:30 in the rain and soon disappeared into the murk. Encountering headwinds, they landed four and a half hours later at Toronto's Century Airport on Dufferin Street, right on the estimate that had been wired ahead by manager O'Brien – a flight that now takes about an hour by airliner.

Landing in gale force winds blowing from the northwest, the "big machine" bounced three times before coming to a stop. Airport attendants ran out and steadied the plane as it taxied slowly towards the hanger. Motorcycle officers were having difficulty holding back the large crowd moving towards the plane. Boyd's first thought was for the safety of the crowd as he pushed his head out of the window repeatedly warning enthusiastic greeters to stay clear of the propeller.

"We are glad to have you home," said Acting Mayor Summerville, "but we're not going to hold you here long for thousands of citizens are waiting to welcome you at the city hall."

Among the greeters were airport manager C.L. Murray and many pilots including James Crang and Ernest French. Captain Earl Hand, president of the Toronto Flying Club, earlier had cancelled plans to send out an escort of welcoming airplanes due to the turbulent, windy weather. Airmen up for short flights that morning had reported intense cold and bumpy conditions with nearby snow showers.

The official greeting party and Boyd family members in fifteen cars were driven quickly through all red lights by a police motorcycle escort to the city hall square, where 10,000 persons had been waiting. Captain Boyd's face was beaming as many stretched forward to shake his hand.

Almost unnoticed except by Boyd was his old nurse, Mrs. Jessie Allcock, who had come to see the boy she once looked after – now a famous flier. When he had come home from the war, she was one of the first to rush madly through the train to welcome him.

Acting Mayor Summerville then gave the official words of welcome and congratulations. He presented Captain Boyd with a cabinet of sterling silver and Lieutenant Connor with an engraved gold wrist watch. In his gracious reply Boyd stressed that the transatlantic flight was a test for greater safety in airplane control in adverse weather conditions. The entire reception was broadcast.

The fliers were overwhelmed with invitations to receptions and club luncheons and to the vice-regal box at the Royal Winter Fair, making the next few days very busy ones. The airmen would lose some of their initial reluctance to speak from public platforms.

A major function was a large dinner at the Royal York Hotel presided over by Earl Hand of the Toronto Flying Club. At the head table were Captain Boyd's father, Police Chief Draper, Mayor Bert Wemp, John Tory and other officials. With many a chuckle and laugh at the grim circumstances which recently seemed to spell death to himself and his gallant navigator, a more relaxed Boyd reviewed the hopes, fears and doubts of his tremendous flight with so many pilots and ex-pilots in the audience.

"Turn the plane into a glider, navigator Connor had suggested when we were 500 miles from land with a blocked fuel tank and insufficient fuel to reach land," Boyd told the crowd. "So we cut the revs to curtail fuel consumption from twelve to about eight gallons an hour and just floated on – but I thought the petrol would give out. I remember my partner telling me to take some altitude, and I said: 'What's the use? You will drown just as much up there as you will down here.' And trying to land in that sea would have just prolonged the agony."

In all the many talks Boyd paid tribute to Connor's navigation skills while Connor said it was Boyd's taking off and landing under most difficult conditions that made their trip successful. They were a great team.

Boyd related that, after their many lengthy delays, they were sitting in the hotel at Harbour Grace when he said: "Come on, Harry, let's go."

"So we went out, met a stranger, and asked him to take us to the field. He drove us there and we got off," Boyd said.

On a more serious note Captain Boyd often concluded: "What Toronto needs is a real airport. I would like to tell people wherever I went that Toronto has the finest airport in the world." With the Great Depression underway, Captain Boyd's hopes were still a few years away.

22

Failed Record Attempts

AFTER CONQUERING the Atlantic Ocean Erroll Boyd sought further adventure and new records to establish. For the next two years the onslaught of the world-wide depression would deter investment in such ventures.

In late 1930 the Argentine Chamber of Commerce offered to pay Boyd expenses of $5,000 for a goodwill trade promotional flight from Canada via Central and South America to Buenos Aires, but arrangements for the flight were never completed.

Erroll Boyd at this time travelled frequently between Canada and the United States, where he was better known as one of the very few transoceanic fliers. While in New York for the 1930 Christmas holiday season, he reported that Canada was keeping pace with world-wide progress in aviation and that her geographic position was favourable for transoceanic flights, both Atlantic and Pacific.

"The jovial airman who piloted the ancient *Columbia* across the Atlantic" was laying plans for a proposed nonstop flight across Canada. He was conferring with friend and adviser J.A. O'Brien and aircraft manufacturer Giuseppe Bellanca about a reliable and faster aircraft.

Earlier plans called for two stops, but Boyd then said: "It's going to be Vancouver to Saint John all in one jump; and I hope to outdo Frank Hawks in his Los Angeles to New York hop."

Always an optimist, he believed the route had sound commercial possibilities. He was a few years too early and, like the South American plans, this experimental long-range flight failed to receive financial support.

Boyd made a leisurely flying trip southward in the old *Columbia* in early 1931 with four passengers: Princess Laura Rospigliosi and John McCormack of New York City, his Prince Edward Island friend Colonel J.S. Jenkins and E. Phillips of Canada. From the airport's restaurant window at Miller Field in Macon, Georgia, they witnessed the crash and death of stunt flyer Johnny Kytle in a Gee Bee Sportster, a racing plane with a barrel-like fuselage.

A month later Boyd was giving many passengers their first flight in the famous *Columbia* from the sand at Daytona Beach at one dollar a head. On March 6, 1931, many newspapers carried a photo of Erroll with millionaire John D. Rockefeller who presented him with eight shiny new dimes, one for each member of his family. The aviator took members of the Rockefeller party for short flights, but the aged and renowned millionaire only "came as near as ever he did to taking an airplane ride," according to the press report.

A minor accident occurred in May. Enroute from Daytona Beach, Florida, to his home in Toronto, Boyd landed his crippled plane in Eastman, Georgia, with three of his children on board. The plane came down on one wheel as part of the landing gear had come loose in midair. The family escaped unhurt. The *Columbia* was grounded for repairs.

Still hungry for adventure, Erroll Boyd planned a sailing trip around the globe from Daytona Beach with boat owner Carl L. Justice and navigator Harry Connor. The thirty-four foot yawl, *Explorer*, with a fourteen hp motor for emergency use, was prepared. Planned to start before the end of 1931, the voyage would attempt to break the record for similar craft set by Harry Pidgeon in 1929 after four years of sailing in the yacht, *Islander*.

Boyd and Justice were making plans while Connor was at sea. A detailed eastbound route of 36,000 miles had been calculated via the Suez and Panama Canals. The trip time was estimated between one and two years. The ship had performed well while sailing from its home port in Washington, D.C. to Florida. With a crew of three, the watches would be four hours on duty and eight hours off.

Justice announced a plan to take pictures and collect data for the Geographic Society. Boyd planned to use some of the *Columbia's* instruments to assist in the navigation and had received marine equipment from business houses interested in the venture. He planned to check and write about airport conditions at their enroute stops.

Much correspondence and arrangement took place regarding food, fuel and supplies. Installation of radio equipment was well under way, and the International Radio Amateurs Association was being alerted.

On November 29 the newly painted *Explorer* sailed smartly down the Halifax River by Daytona Beach as cameras flashed and yachts saluted. It was a trial run to stretch her new rigging. In addition to Justice and Boyd, the latter's wife and two small daughters were on board. But the circumnavigation of the globe failed to materialize as, late in the planning stages, one member of the trio found it impossible to stay away so long from his regular employment.

In 1932 Captain Erroll Boyd was the only Canadian aviator invited to go to Rome as guest of the Royal Italian Aero Club conference in May. Although the *Columbia* was undergoing maintenance repairs, he hoped it would be available for a solo flight from Harbour Grace, Newfoundland, nonstop to Rome.

If successful, Boyd would become the first man to span the North Atlantic twice by plane and the second to fly it solo, the other being Lindbergh. His friends hoped that the Canadian government might provide some aid to enable Canadian representation at the conclave of

Yacht for proposed round-world trip, 1931 (Courtesy of Boyd family)

famous aviators but it was not to be. The aircraft was not yet in top shape and the financial backing did not exist.

In the summer of 1932 Boyd's seven-year-old plane was undergoing extensive modifications at the Bellanca factory in Newcastle, Delaware. The press learned that Boyd was seeking funds to finance the first solo round-the-world flight, one year before Wiley Post achieved this record.

Erroll's daughter Bey, then fourteen, pleasantly recalls the summer of 1932 as the year her father sang his Broadway hit song, *Dreams*, at a recital at St. Mildred's College, Toronto. She said her dad often played the piano during their growing up years, including a special exercise he had composed when eight years old.

Before leaving Toronto for a little lobbying in Ottawa, Boyd indicated his preference to start the flight in his birthplace, Toronto.

"Some people forget that I am a Canadian travelling with a British passport," the optimistic airman told the press. "Encircling the globe would bring Canada to the fore."

Not having much luck interesting financial backers for his solo effort, he later placed a prominent advertisement in a New York paper seeking a companion for the non-stop portion to Europe who would invest $8,000. He would now take a passenger as far as Berlin and then continue solo, planning a route across China to Tokyo and then the short route across the Pacific by way of the Aleutian Islands and Alaska.

Wiley Post and his Australian-born navigator, Harold Gatty, had circled the globe in just under nine days in the previous year, 1931, in the more powerful and better financed Lockheed Vega *Winnie Mae*. Post wrote shortly afterwards that aviation needed something original to stimulate the then infant air passenger business, and this, too, was Boyd's ambition.

Having spent much of the summer planning for this flight, Boyd admitted at one point that the preparatory work was worse than the flight itself. The advertisement had produced no serious replies and sufficient financial backing was not available. He then considered a less ambitious alternative.

Reports from Roosevelt Field, Long Island, in September revealed that plans were underway for two ocean flights. One would be a flight by Boyd and Connor in the *Columbia* to Moscow. The other was being engineered by Roger Q. Williams to a point east of Istanbul, Turkey, to break the distance record established by Russell Boardman and John Polando. They had flown the more than 5,000 miles non-stop from New York to Istanbul a year earlier, 1931, in the Bellanca *Cape Cod*. Neither of these two flights materialized due to financial delays and approaching winter weather, which made the attempts inadvisable.

With the *Columbia* completely overhauled, Boyd had considered at one point an attempt on the solo endurance record of thirty-six hours in conjunction with the Canadian National Exhibition in Toronto.

During the winter of 1932-33 Erroll Boyd completed the organization of an aerial company, President Airlines, Inc., of which he was president. Round-the-world flier Clyde Pangborn was vice-president and Robert G. Lyon its secretary. In spite of the depression, Boyd finally would achieve success in obtaining financial support the following summer for a new record-breaking flight.

23

Record Flight to Caribbean

THE YEAR 1933 would prove to be a better one for Erroll Boyd. By the summer he and two companions took the eight-year-old *Columbia* on a pioneering travel promotion flight from Floyd Bennett Field, New York, to Port-au-Prince, Haiti, and return.

On the evening before departure the sponsors of this goodwill flight held a testimonial dinner to meet the crew and Haiti's consul-general in New York. With Boyd on this venture were Robert G. Lyon, ex-navy flier, as co-pilot and Harold P. Davis, author-observer who once worked for a Haitian newspaper and had published a history of Haiti, *Black Democracy*.

Among the 5,000 persons who cheered the *Columbia's* take-off from New York at 3:35 p.m. on June 11 were Bert Acosta and Porter Moore. Acosta, along with Clarence Chamberlain, had set a world endurance record in the same plane in 1927. Porter Moore was Boyd's flight organizer. Erroll carried a pet turtle named Bozie as a good luck token. It had been sent to him by his two youngest daughters, Honor and Virginia, who were attending school in Toronto. There they were under the good care of his parents and sister Dorothy.

The plan was to complete the flight in twenty-four hours and return via Washington. The route selected was via Atlantic City and along the east coast to Florida, and then over Cuba to Haiti, a total distance of more than 2,400 miles, a greater distance than the over-water mileage from Newfoundland to Ireland. With 400 gallons of fuel on board Boyd took off in about 2,700 feet.

The plane carried a box of flowers and rose petals for Boyd to drop over Cuba in memory of Wilmer Stultz who made a nonstop flight to Havana in the *Columbia* in 1928. For food the fliers took two broiled chickens, two gallons of water, two quarts of coffee and a quart of lemon juice.

Some fear for their safety was expressed in the media when they were not sighted by Havana the next morning.

"Erroll has been flying so long that we are no longer worried when he makes a long trip," Boyd's mother told the *Toronto Star*. She continued:

> And, of course, the Columbia is such a wonderful ship. When Erroll made his trans-Atlantic flight, Captain Hand told me it was the greatest of all trans-Atlantic flights. For that time of the year, and in the Columbia, which everyone called 'an old crate', it was quite miraculous.
>
> Erroll will come out all right, just as he has in the past. The day he was shot down overseas, I knew something had happened before I ever got official word. I told my husband, 'Something has happened'. I was up in the morning before the cable from the admiralty reported him missing. Even then, I was sure he was safe.

But disaster almost struck Boyd on this occasion. Climbing to clear some small mountains near St. Marc, about sixty miles short of their destination of Port-au-Prince, the engine sputtered and quit, probably due to water in the gasoline. The *Columbia* was forced down in the afternoon in some mud flats after twenty-four hours in the air. Calling it a remarkable landing, Davis said "an error of twenty-five feet would have resulted in wreckage of the plane in a deep ditch." They had completed the first flight from New York to Haiti, if slightly short of their destination.

The stranded airmen sent five messengers to St. Marc to telephone the capital, Port-au-Prince, where the district engineer arranged a rescue party.

"We had the most miserable night I have ever spent," co-pilot Bob Lyon reported. "The persistent mosquitoes made sleep impossible."

At 3 a.m. the next morning, almost twelve hours after their landing, the rescue party reached them "with beer and sandwiches."

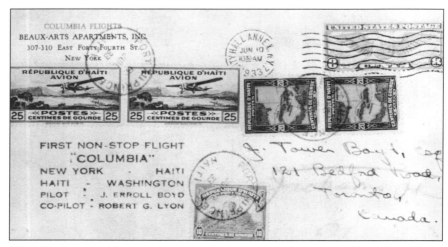

Haiti postcard with valuable stamps (Courtesy of Boyd family)

With the aid of about forty local people, they got the ship out of the muck and up on higher ground after daylight. The men cleared a path to provide Erroll barely adequate space for take-off. After some fifteen hours in the tropical jungle they departed and landed at Bowen Field at 7:30 a.m. to a huge reception.

After a quick bath, shave and breakfast, they were received on June 13 by the mayor at 10:00 a.m. In addition to the presentation of gifts, the mayor even promised to name a street Boyd Avenue, all of this after much champagne.

The crew was then greeted at the presidential palace with more speeches and champagne. President Vincente decorated them with the Medal of Honour and Merit, Erroll with the highest grade, Chevalier. They were also received by the U.S. minister, Mr. Armour, Haiti being under Marine Corps occupation. After more than two days without sleep, they sank into their luxurious beds in a hotel floor reserved for their use.

Bob Lyon said in his report that Erroll took the president for his first airplane ride, even though his aides tried to discourage him, and "he liked it." Lyon added that they had also been invited to adjacent Santo Domingo by its president.

The return voyage was delayed as Boyd and Davis were stricken with tropical fever. They then waited for favourable weather reports and finally took off on the late afternoon of July 5 hoping to make Washington in sixteen hours nonstop. It became the toughest flight in Boyd's career.

The *Washington Herald* reported: "Thirty-two seconds were required for a takeoff from a 1500-foot runway. The ship was loaded with 300 gallons of gasoline."

After about three hours they encountered the most amazing mixture of thundershowers and electrical storms Boyd had ever seen, much worse than his transatlantic flight in the same ship. Their altitude varied from 50 feet to 7,000 feet.

They sighted the lights of a ship and flew around it for about three hours waiting for the weather to improve. Seeing clearer weather to the south they proceeded and soon passed the lights of Havana. As the weather was improving, they headed for the mainland, touching the shore at Key West. They made a short, unplanned stopover at noon at Savannah, Georgia, to refuel and arrived a little weary at Washington's Hoover Airport in the late afternoon of July 6.

There followed a reception at the Haitian Embassy and visits to the White House and to Postmaster General James Farley. Air mail had been carried both to and from Haiti. Boyd carried a special message from President Stenio Vincente of Haiti to President Franklin D. Roosevelt. For Mrs. Roosevelt there was a gift of special coffee, grown at an altitude of 6,000 feet.

The Haitian minister, the erudite Dr. Bellegarde, commented on the coincidental landing at Savannah, the city where 800 Haitians had fought under French Compte d'Estaing for American independence, of which the airmen were undoubtedly unaware.

The grand old *Columbia* returned to New York and then to Toronto via Buffalo in mid-July. Before going to Toronto, Boyd and Lyon made a short flying visit to the soaring field at Elmira, N.Y. where they received much acclaim. The press reported that the famous aviator, commenting on gliders, said he would "stick to something he knows, such as transoceanic flights, solo endurance contests and the like."

Boyd was interviewed extensively by the Buffalo press about this time. He referred to his first airplane ride with Lincoln Beachey who had been the first to fly under the bridge at Niagara Falls.

"Which reminds me," grinned the captain, "we did a little under-the-bridge flying on our trip from New York . . . Out of New York we hit a heavy fog and were forced to fly under the George Washington and Bear Mountain bridges on the Hudson."

After a forty-minute hop from Buffalo, Boyd landed at Toronto's Barker airport on Dufferin Street, accompanied by his attractive wife and Bob Lyon, co-pilot on his Haiti flight. As the good-natured and debonair Boyd rolled from the cockpit to kiss his daughters, Bey and Kathleen, one asked, "Where's mother?" A quick check revealed that, in the excitement of the arrival, Mrs. Boyd had been left to struggle out from behind the gasoline tank on her own. The space was less than a foot wide. A happy band of helpers soon fixed that.

A reporter, describing Boyd as a carefree flier happy with a couple of wings and an engine, asked him, as he shook off the loved ones, "But about that Haiti flight?"

"Toughest I was ever on," he said. "We ran into the tail end of that West Indian hurricane on the trip back that killed twelve people in Jamaica. We took off from Port au Prince and struck dirty weather right off. Ran into thunderstorms and everything . . . we circled over a ship for three hours. It was 'soup' right down to the water."

The reporter then asked a question put to him by a former British war ace: "Why is it, when Canada's airmen during the war were admittedly second to none, that Canada seems to take so little interest in aviation now?"

"I don't know," he replied. "I wish I did know," he came back a little desperately when pressed. "I tried for three years to get a job here. I couldn't. I'd rather be here. They'll have to take an interest in it soon."

Around the time of Boyd's record Haiti flight, other aviation events were making the headlines. Two Spaniards, Barberan and Collar, completed one of the longest over-water flights from Spain to Cuba in just under forty hours. James Mattern was down in Siberia on his solo round-the-world attempt. General Balbo and an armada of twenty-four planes and ninety-six men were enroute in easy stages from Italy to the Chicago World's Fair.

In 1940, some seven years after the Haiti flight, Erroll Boyd's good friend, Bob Lyon, died in New York. After the appropriate ceremony, Erroll took Bob Lyon's ashes aloft in a U.S. Navy aircraft and scattered them in the area. It was the only time Boyd ever flew with a parachute.

Many years later in the 1950s, Erroll Boyd exchanged letters with retired postmaster Farley regarding first flight covers commemorating the Haiti flight, some of which are held at the Smithsonian Institute in Washington. They are very valuable today.

24

Jobs Were Scarce

DURING his life Erroll Boyd must have commuted between Toronto and New York many hundreds of times. With his partner, Robert Lyon, he stopped over briefly in Buffalo on July 14, 1933, enroute to New York from Toronto where the captain had been visiting two of his young daughters, Bey and Kathleen. The press reports revealed not only the fame of the *Columbia*, but also Boyd's accurate predictions of future air travel.

The reports eloquently described the *Columbia*, queen of all airplanes – the stately veteran, the silver wings of which have written history in the skies of three continents, carrying two smiling pilots fresh from charting the airway from New York to Port-au-Prince, Haiti.

The first visit of Captain Boyd to Buffalo in many years and the first visit of the great *Columbia* in four years had created a ripple of excitement among fliers and air folk. They hurried to view the great plane, la belle *Columbia*, which rivalled the *Spirit of St. Louis*, then resting in the Smithsonian, and to shake the hands of its pilots.

The press reported the great plane was the pride and joy of its owner and refuted the claims of Amelia Earhart and other experts that the 'life' of a record-making plane was only four years. The media listed in detail the *Columbia's* achievements, summarized on the side of the aircraft.

"Scheduled air flying over the Atlantic is positively coming," Boyd told them.

> Lindbergh is now mapping one air lane for Pan-American Airways. Five years from now the planes will

hop off for England like they do now for New York from Buffalo.

If you could see those great airliners coming in at various coast ports in South America, crowded with passengers, you would realize that the North Atlantic regular run is simply a next step, and not an undertaking fraught with danger.

The route taken by Balboa will not be the commercial air lane, in my estimation. That route is too far north and too dangerous when winter sets in. The hop will be from Canada to Newfoundland straight across to Ireland and then down into England, France and other European terminals.

Boyd was only one year out in his five-year forecast, as both Pan American and Imperial Airways inaugurated scheduled transatlantic flying boat service in 1939 just before the outbreak of World War II. He also predicted the use of emergency weather station ships to provide navigation and communication guidance, the establishment of which were delayed due to the war. Boyd mentioned that the *Columbia* would be a featured exhibit at the Chicago World's Fair later that summer.

In August 1933, the *Toronto Star* reported that Captain Boyd and his famous aircraft would attempt to break the solo flight endurance record over Toronto's Canadian National Exhibition, the world's largest annual fair. The existing record on the books of the F.A.I. of Paris – the controlling organization for international aviation competition – was thirty-six hours and eleven minutes.

The aircraft, then hangared at Toronto's Barker Field, had already flown non-stop longer than that, therefore the attempt would be more an endurance test of the pilot rather than the machine. Considering the strain, the monotony and the numbing, incessant roar of the motor, Boyd said "that would be long enough for any man."

Also in August Boyd and his wife and the famous *Columbia* were special guests in Montreal as some 25,000 persons paid admission at St. Hubert airport for the 5th Canadian Air Pageant. The pageant featured an exhibition of aerobatics by the British-built RCAF Siskin machines from Trenton. Bad weather unfortunately prevented a huge formation of seventy-five aircraft from leaving Roosevelt Field, Long Island, N.Y.

The special guest of honour at this flying pageant was Amy Johnson Mollison, billed as "the world's foremost aviatrix." As Amy Johnson she became the first woman to make a solo flight from England to Australia in 1930 in nineteen days in an open cockpit biplane. In Australia she met Jim Mollison, an airline pilot with Charles Kingsford-Smith's Australian National Airways.

Jim Mollison first came into the public eye in 1931 when he flew from Australia to England in less than nine days. He later made a record flight to South Africa and became the first person to solo both North and South Atlantic.

Jim and Amy Mollison took off from Pendine Sands, Wales, in their de Havilland 84 Dragon twin-engine biplane called *Seafarer* on July 22, 1933 with Floyd Bennett Field on Long Island as their destination. They crash-landed about fifty-five miles short of their goal at Stratford Airport near Bridgeport, Conn. Because of headline publicity, an estimated 7,000 cars of sightseers were parked in the area within two hours, and the *Seafarer* was ripped apart by souvenir seekers. Such was the excitement caused by transatlantic exploits in this era.

In spite of their injuries the Mollisons shortened their hospital stay to thirty hours knowing an official reception was waiting for them in New York. And some reception it was! On August 1, an estimated 200,000 people lining a ticker-tape parade greeted the first husband and wife team to fly from Europe. In New York, Erroll Boyd organized a special luncheon to honour Jimmy, while Amelia Earhart hosted Amy.

Unlike the Boyd-Connor lifetime friendship, most flying teams of the era broke up. The Mollisons separated in 1935 and divorced in 1938. Amy died in England during the war in early 1941 while ferrying a twin-engine Airspeed Oxford. Jim died a broken man in a nursing home in 1959, an alcoholic unable to handle the transition away from the limelight.

The Canadian air pageant also featured other pilots who had flown the Atlantic, including round-the-world flier Clyde Pangborn and group captain E.W. Stedman, acting controller of civil aviation in Ottawa, who crossed from St. Hubert to Cardington, England, on board the airship R-100 in 1930. Famous speed racer Frank Hawks was among the many pilots participating.

This very same week Boyd's first accident in sixteen years would prevent his planned record endurance attempt. The incident took place in the early evening near his parents' summer home on Lake Simcoe. He was taking off from George Metcalfe's field one mile west of Sutton, Ontario, on a short flight to Toronto for a speaking engagement with the Toronto Kiwanians the next day. The previous day he and his wife had flown back from the Montreal air meet.

"Erroll started the motor up and thought she was running all right," Mr. Boyd, Sr. related. "He got about ten feet in the air, and then it nosed down to the ground and nearly turned over nose first. Erroll came rolling out of the cabin. I could see he was afraid of fire. When he started to run, I knew he wasn't badly hurt."

When the reporters from the *Toronto Star* visited him later, Boyd was dancing at his oldest daughter's party at her grandfather's place, and actually seemed jubilant about the whole thing. The only evidence of minor injury were some light bandages on his forehead.

"I certainly had it coming to me," Boyd laughed. "It's my first smash-up since 1917 and perhaps I was due for one."

Boyd took the reporters to the field where farmer Metcalfe kept watch over sightseers in search of souvenirs and to prevent smoking near leaking gasoline. The Bellanca was standing on its nose almost upside down with tail up in the air. It was supported in this position by a rail fence upon which it was resting so easily it didn't move a rail. The left wing had suffered minor damage from a small tree and the propeller was broken. Boyd assured them it would be on hand later in the week for an appearance at the Canadian National Exhibition.

A brief news report a few days later revealed that souvenir hunters had removed parts from the famous monoplane while on display at this annual exhibition while the guards were explaining the plane's record to spectators! Between here and at Sutton, the site of the accident, gas and oil caps, part of the instrument panel, a windshield and aviation watch were pilfered. Boyd commented crisply, "I would like to keep some of the plane."

Shortly after this accident Boyd's five-year-old niece, Mary Macrae Gooch, enjoyed a visit from her famous uncle. Boyd still had a patch on his forehead from the accident. Some six decades later she remembered: "He gave me such a hearty hug and kiss because he was such a lively, buoyant individual – much like my grandmother – a person you would long remember."

Towards the end of 1933, Erroll, his wife and four daughters were resident at the Beaux Arts apartments back in New York City where the prospects for earning a living from aviation might be better.

"I am still dragging a living out of aviation," the soft spoken Canadian told a New York columnist. "My family and I are not hungry. I fly hither, thither and yon when people hire me to do it."

With both a creative mind and contacts in the entertainment world, Erroll gave a lot of thought to the development of a movie or play to dramatize all the romance, triumphs, tragic failures and heroism that had gone into the aeronautical conquests of the last few years. It would feature the story of the record-breaking *Columbia*, possibly the most famous plane of its era.

Boyd was working on the arrangements for such a production with Hal Skelly, well known actor and author. In his colourful career Skelly had been involved in the circus, opera and musical comedy. He played with such people as John Barrymore and Leon Errol. For a while he turned to prize-fighting and pro baseball, and then back to show business. Playing in *Burlesque* with Barbara Stanwyck was the peak of Skelly's career. He played later in several motion pictures, and was also a sportsman aviator.

A double tragedy occurred to block this worthy initiative. First, Hal Skelly was killed suddenly when his car was struck by a train at a level crossing near Cornwall, Connecticut. Second, the famous *Columbia* was mostly destroyed in a hangar fire at the location of the Bellanca factory in Newcastle, Delaware, on January 25, 1934.

Another project of Boyd's was shattered. Erroll, forever the optimist, said part of the plane was saved, and that it could be reproduced from plans still extant. Four other ships were destroyed in the fire caused by sparks from a nearby grass fire. Bellanca officials estimated the loss at $250,000.

In early 1934 the Boyd family were lodged in Fort Lauderdale for the remainder of the winter. In addition to his flying, Erroll soon picked up a job as aviation editor of the *Miami Beach Tribune*. It was in this role that Boyd covered the inaugural arrival of Eastern Airline's Douglas DC-2 – piloted by war ace Eddie Rickenbacker – in Miami. The DC-2 was a forerunner to the DC-3, and a milestone in aviation progress. Boyd later became president of the Tribune Flying Club and broadcast frequent aviation programs over Miami radio station WQAM.

A report from Miami dated December 15, 1934, said Captain

Erroll Boyd, Toronto transatlantic flier, won another bout with death in the sky. Flying from Miami to Jacksonville with three passengers, Boyd was caught in a sudden storm and was forced to turn back, flying blind. His engine went dead and when he tried to start it again it backfired, enveloping the machine in flames. The captain manoeuvred the burning ship to the landing field in time to extinguish the flames before any serious damage resulted.

"Tell the folks back home that I am still a Canadian," Boyd told the *Toronto Star Weekly* representative. "My only reason for not returning to Canada to live is the uncertainty of securing steady employment in the field of commercial aviation."

In early 1935 many advertisements appeared urging people to see Miami from the air and to fly with transatlantic flier Erroll Boyd, and to attend the regular weekly broadcast and party sponsored by Tribune Flying Club members.

In the mid-1930s Erroll Boyd became private pilot for Charles G. "Abe" Lincoln, Jr., nationally known president of the Virginia-Lincoln Furniture Company of Marion, Virginia. Once, while stopped over in Houston, Lincoln told the press that business conditions were improving everywhere he'd been! This was optimism in the middle of the Depression! Boyd and Lincoln made a trip to Boyd's old territory in Mexico. Old photos in Boyd's files indicate the Bellanca 140 force-landed without damage on a high plateau about nine or ten thousand feet above sea level in the mountains some eighty miles from Mexico City.

In early 1936 Boyd considered an attempt to eclipse the airplane altitude mark of 47,000 feet held by two Italian aviators. He planned to use a 450 hp supercharged Wasp five-passenger cabin plane for the flight, presumably a Bellanca Skyrocket, but no record exists of this attempt having been completed.

In May of 1935, *Gold*, the mining magazine of Canada's north, produced a special edition featuring aviation. In it there appeared a guest article by Erroll Boyd about his 1930 transatlantic flight with the title, "My navigator proved his wonderful ability."

The magazine's editor prefaced it with the following remarks:

> Thus does Erroll Boyd characteristically pay unselfish
> tribute to his partner in the closing paragraph of his
> personal account of their transatlantic flight. Erroll Boyd

was the first and only Canadian to fly the Atlantic. His reception in Toronto following that historic episode had all the spontaneity of a salvo of wet firecrackers on a rainy day. After all, Lindbergh was not the first, he was the first American. But Boyd was merely a Canadian. Had he been a British aristocrat or a Hollywood movie star, Toronto's citizenry would have struck up the bands, run up the flags and showered the streets with ticket tape. His flight, made late in October, through fog the greater part of the way, was one of the most epic ocean hops on record. They risked all, he and his partner, Harry Connor, with no thought of gain other than "the realization of a long cherished dream."

The mining editor was writing in a period when Torontonians and citizens of Canada were only slowly moving away from a colonial mentality, and at a time when they lacked a strong sense of national identity. Canada seemed to have no heroes of its own even though the U.S. press often referred to Erroll Boyd as the Lindbergh of Canada.

25

At the Depth of the Depression

THE YEAR 1937 was not a good one financially for the Boyd family, then living in Toronto. It was two years before the outbreak of World War II and two years before the inauguration of transcontinental passenger service by Trans-Canada Air Lines, nearly a decade behind such development in the U.S.A. Boyd was 45, at that time considered old for a pilot.

Canada had suffered badly from the Depression and lack of any coordinated air policy by the Bennett government earlier in the decade. The nation lacked airline connections between major population centres, unlike many other countries.

On June 12 a story in the *Toronto Star* written by its ace reporter Gregory Clark was captioned: "Toronto Aviator Who Flew Across the Atlantic Gets Eviction Notice from Bailiff."

The story began that Captain Erroll Boyd, the only Canadian who had yet flown the Atlantic, had in his time received many interesting and curious pieces of paper. One, for example, commissioned him with the rank of general in the army of Haiti. Another was a pilot's licence dated 1915. But the strangest piece of paper in all his adventurous life was the blue piece that he received the previous day evicting him from his home and seizing his possessions.

Clark summarized many of Boyd's achievements and mentioned that the transatlantic flyer of 1930 had gained $38,000 from that single achievement, much of it used for the expenses involved. Following his return to Canada from that flight, everybody told Boyd he should settle down.

"To what?" asked Captain Boyd expectantly. His kinsman, Sir

George Perley, said to him: "Erroll, when are you going to give up this perilous business and settle down to earth?"

Captain Boyd believed this question from a distinguished fellow-Canadian summarized the negative attitude of Canada towards aviation. The biggest peril of flying in Canada was the danger of going hungry or maybe earning a few dollars in the remote and lonely northern regions, hardly the way to raise a large family. Boyd had hoped his move to Toronto would coincide with a new awakening in Canada for the potential of the flying business.

"Were you worried over your kids," Clark asked him over a coffee "when you saw that vast, dangerous ocean under you about half-way across?"

"Do you know," said Boyd, startled, "the first time I have been worried about my children was yesterday." And he looked into space with an expression of astonishment. "And I suppose," he said quietly, "they've often been pretty worried about me."

Such a sweet apology to the young ladies! Probably Captain Boyd can get a lift from any one of his many well-to-do friends, Clark wrote. But unfortunately, he not merely won't but can't do that. Being an eagle, you can't cluck like a hen. So Gregory Clark said to him: "When we heard of this blue paper, we thought there was a story in it. You know, 'Famous pilot crashed by bailiff.' But somehow the story has all died in us. What can we do for you?"

"What," asked Boyd with a wry smile, "can you do?"

"Well, we could write a kind of a story about how you did this and that . . . no apple sauce, no gravy," replied Clark.

"I've had a lot of publicity," said Captain Boyd. "I'm tough."

So Gregory Clark wrote the story.

The day after this story, Gregory Clark also wrote E.L. Cousins, general manager of the Toronto Harbour Commission, which was beginning construction of the Island Airport. He wrote:

> We have been trying to help Erroll Boyd get a place
> in Canada. So have others . . . He has just had a
> disappointment in that Senator O'Connor can't do
> anything for him . . . Erroll is completely broke . . . It has
> just occurred to me that on top of his long and
> distinguished record, his high competence as a flyer, his
> experience, wide enough with newspapers like ours, that

there might be an immediate job in connection with the airport project . . . maybe in publicity, public relations and news control . . . There will be a goodly amount of 'bushwa' written with increasing velocity as the project advances, and it will be a little sounder, more colorful, and still controllable coming from a man who happens to be a captain, a transatlantic flyer and a Canadian . . . I for one would see a feather in your hat if you could place Boyd.

While there is no record of the response, Erroll Boyd later that year and throughout 1938 became aviation editor and columnist for the *Toronto Star* and its prestigious *Star Weekly*, and received many more assignments from them. Some of his reports and opinions shed an interesting light on events leading to scheduled air service in the area. His column, "Wings Over Toronto," often dealt with wings over Canada and the world.

Some of Boyd's predictions were quite accurate. For example, he foresaw the arrival of a 600 mph aircraft linking Toronto with London, England, in five or six hours. He predicted that the increasing volume of air traffic would lower fares making them competitive with other forms of transportation. He predicted a safety factor greater than that of automobiles. He publicized the fact that even then, a U.S. passenger could purchase a $5,000 insurance policy at the airport for twenty-five cents.

In spite of his very strong advocacy of air travel, Erroll Boyd was no fan of lighter-than-air craft. The day after the disastrous explosion of the *Hindenburg* at Lakehurst, New Jersey in 1937, he regretted the serious loss of life put down to pioneering. But he strongly expressed his opinion that lighter-than-air craft were not practical as proven by numerous accidents. He attributed the accident to static electricity igniting one of the sixteen gas cells.

In the case of war Boyd said these big gas-bags costing well over a million dollars would be a pawn in a fight with a $10,000 aeroplane. If the powers decided to build more, helium or some other non-flammable gas would be used.

"The Germans no doubt will put up a strong argument that if the U.S. would have sold them helium, this latest tragedy would not have happened," he said. "On the other hand, the Germans have always argued hydrogen is much more profitable, due to its low price and lifting power. On the *Hindenburg* the officers and crew had to wear felt overshoes, precautions to avoid static which would ignite hydrogen immediately."

Boyd attributed the number of safe Zeppelin crossings to Dr. Hugo Eckener's efforts at avoiding storms and rough air which would provide great strain on an airship over 800 feet long. Boyd attributed the *Macon* and *Akron* disasters to such weather. He felt Great Britain knew when to stop as they had not forgotten the R-101 tragedy which occurred just before the arrival of Boyd's 1930 flight in England.

On the visit of the Imperial Airways flying boat *Cambria* to Toronto harbor in 1937, Boyd expressed the hope that its presence would accelerate the development of Toronto's two planned air terminals at Malton and the downtown island.

Boyd battled red tape. One example he used was that of A.F. "Sandy" MacDonald, who many pilots will recall as the initiator of the bible of Canadian student pilots, *From the Ground Up*. By landing at Pontiac, Michigan, on a business trip, MacDonald had incurred a questionable customs penalty of $500.

The delay caused MacDonald, in returning to Canada, to grope for a landing at the Toronto Flying Club field as darkness was rapidly approaching. Boyd urged the need of a properly lit airport.

In spite of all this, Captain Boyd was a loyal Toronto booster. He wrote:

> Toronto's prospects as an airways centre are creating jealousy and alarm in Montreal. Toronto has the go-getter spirit that will make her what she's determined to be: Metropolis of Canada.

At that time, of course, Montreal was Canada's largest and number one city. Since then the situation has reversed.

About this time in October 1937 United Airlines was planning to send one of its new DC-3 Sky Lounge Mainliners to Toronto and Montreal on a promotional trip. The U.S. Department of Commerce intervened and cancelled the Toronto landing because of the unavailability of adequate runways, but did approve the Montreal landing at St. Hubert airport.

Towards the end of 1937, transport minister C.D. Howe mentioned that the Toronto Island site would be used eighty-five per cent of the time and Malton only fifteen per cent when the island could not be used due to bad weather. Erroll Boyd, in what proved to be correct, contradicted the minister and said that within two years with the larger planes Malton would be used practically 100 per cent of the time. On an early inspection of the proposed site at Malton, Boyd wrote that he had to drive his car slowly enough "to hold my seat without going through the roof." Three years later when the author first visited the airport, the road was still not paved!

26

The Plight of Pioneer Pilots

WHILE Boyd was writing his "Wings Over Toronto," the competing *Toronto Telegram* carried "Cloud Combing" by Percy T. Cole. Without reference to Boyd's early transatlantic flight of 1930, Cole presented some interesting figures on transatlantic flying prior to 1937:

- How many airplanes tried to get across the Atlantic? 90
- How many got where they were going? 12
- How many got across some way or other? 30
- How many haven't landed yet? 39
- How many came back without crossing? 9
- How many lost their lives in the attempts? 41

Such statistics may not be too reliable due to the difficulty of defining the North and South Atlantic, but certainly point out the dangers of such flights.

When Erroll Boyd was at the peak of his financial problems in 1937, another famous long-distance flier, Amy Johnson Mollison, spoke of the money background to romantic, glamorous flights.

"Before my Australian flight in 1930," she said, "I began with exactly nothing. After seven years I return to almost the same position, but with a wealth of experience and memories money could never buy."

The approximate cost of her flight from England to Australia in 1930 was about $6,000 as she paid only $3,000 for her second-hand Gipsy Moth. Gas, oil, plugs and parachute were supplied free.

She received one big payment of $10,000 for the exclusive story of her flight, and spoke about other sources of revenue for pioneer pilots. Some friends give gifts and other revenue can come from exhibition of the airplane, endorsement of products, writing a book or making personal appearances on the value of your name as news, she said. Once the flight is over, though, a pilot was expected to live in a better life style.

"After a time you get restless and want to repeat those hectic days of adventure, danger and thrills," she said. "Your original record has been broken many times so you now require a faster, more expensive machine. The financing is more difficult and the insurance is prohibitive."

Even with a successful second flight, the returns are often less. Amy Johnson Mollison said most of the long-distance record pilots who were flying during the years of 1930 to 1935 made big money, but few of them had much left in 1937.

"Not all of it had been squandered on easy living, luxurious clothes, cocktail parties and the like, as is popularly supposed," she said. Most of it had gone in expenses and liabilities which were not as well known as the gifts and prize money received. After one of her record flights in which she was supposed to have pocketed thousands, Amy actually left with $250 in cash which was owed in taxes. After another record flight she received bills for medical expenses and a bill for the cost of her own reception. Fame and fortune made overnight soon fades away, but the pilot retains a golden hoard of memories.

As far as making money is concerned, most of the transatlantic flights were dismal financial failures. The notable contradiction was the first solo hop made by Charles Lindbergh who reportedly became a millionaire. Amelia Earhart, America's foremost woman flier, and Commander Richard E. Byrd also reaped a rich harvest from their record flights. These were the exceptions as most pioneer transatlantic airmen ran into very little easy money.

Many flights bred bitter quarrels over money. Clarence Chamberlain who flew the Atlantic two weeks behind Lindbergh claimed millionaire Charles Levine, his passenger, never paid him the $25,000 he had promised.

The early successful pioneer distance fliers were primarily good aviators with relatively little experience or interest in business principles or corporate organization. The first transpacific pilot, Clyde Pangborn, provides an example.

Boyd's friend and business partner in the early 1930s, Pangborn had been half-owner and chief pilot of what was probably the greatest barnstorming organization of all time – the Gates Flying Circus. It had thrilled millions of people with its spectacular stunts in the 1920s. The brains behind the crazy promotions and death-defying feats was the heavy-drinking eccentric, Ivan Gates. Pangborn and Gates had nothing in common and had completely opposite personalities, but Pangborn implicitly trusted Gates' wife, Hazel, who managed the finances.

Pangborn's later record 1931 transpacific flight was financed primarily by co-pilot Hugh Herndon's wealthy mother. Before the flight Pangborn had signed – without reading it first – a document that Herndon thrust in front of him. Although Pangborn provided the planning, brains and skill behind the world-girdling flight, he did not receive his expected fifty per cent but only ten per cent of the $25,000 prize money. Furthermore, he discovered later that he was barred for a full year from making any personal appearances, endorsing any products, or doing any promotion related to the flight. Not surprisingly, Clyde Pangborn and Hugh Herndon broke up over money.

Even when he was later with Erroll Boyd and Bob Lyon as vice-president of President Air Lanes, Pangborn exhibited little interest in anything other than directly flying. He flew as co-pilot to Roscoe Turner in an United Airlines Boeing 247-D, finishing third overall in "the world's greatest air race" from England to Australia in 1934. During the war he flew some 170 Atlantic and Pacific flights for the Ferry Command. Today the airport in his home of Wenatchee, Washington, is named after him.

While Boyd had more business experience than most early pioneers, he found the planning details arduous. It is interesting to note that the details for two of his more successful ventures – his transatlantic hop and his flight to Haiti – were organized by O'Brien and Porter Moore respectively.

Edward Schlee and William Brock attempted a world flight in a Stinson Detroiter monoplane in August 1927, and flew from Detroit eastbound as far as Tokyo. Schlee acknowledged resentment against the city of Detroit for having to pay $2,700 out of his own pocket for a public banquet at which he was guest of honour. Wiley Post was nearly penniless when he died with Will Rogers in a crash in Alaska in September 1935. Roger Q. Williams and L. Yancey reportedly made not a nickel on their New York to Rome flight in 1929.

But none who lived regretted their efforts.

27

Helping Youth to Succeed

IN EARLY 1938 Captain Erroll Boyd organized the Aviation Scouts of Canada, a forerunner of the air cadet movement, to promote the interests of aviation in all its forms. Boyd embarked on this non-profit venture without any government aid following his difficult financial year, which shows his dedication to aviation and to youth.

In the very first issue of its paper February 1, 1938, he outlined the goal of the Aviation Scouts of Canada: To provide assistance and help to both the young and old to gather some inside knowledge of this new business of flying. Boyd said the Aviation Scouts of Canada would try to give a true picture of aviation in all its forms. The early issues showed that a number of celebrities had signified their cooperation by becoming Honorary Members of Aviation Scouts. These included Billie Bishop, Sir Malcolm Campbell, Leigh Brintnell, Jim Crang, Howard Hughes, Lowell Thomas, Roscoe Turner, Sir Hubert Wilkins and well known politicians.

Dale Carnegie, another honourary member, advertised his famous book, How to Win Friends and Influence People, under which Boyd added a footnote that the aviation scouts could learn more in five minutes by reading this book than if they read the funny papers for five months.

One article in the paper revealed that members of the Montreal Light Aeroplane Club had logged over 1,000 hours in 1937 without a single accident, an insignificant figure by present standards. Also described was an improved air traffic control landing system for cross-wind landings developed by Stuart Graham. The paper reported that TWA carried 90,000 passengers on scheduled flights in 1937 – a volume easily carried by a single airliner today!

A feature called Wingovers outlined many short items which illustrate the state of flying in this period:

+ American airline aircraft would soon be required to carry radio compasses or direction finders on all their planes.
+ To guide airmen, the names of 145 cities and towns in South Africa were placed on station roofs along 6,000 miles of railway lines.
+ Germany planned to resume her transatlantic dirigible service using non-explosive American helium gas in the spring. The LZ-130 was expected to replace the lost Hindenburg in regular service between Germany and the U.S.A. in May.
+ Great Britain had organized a balloon barrage for air defence.
+ Eight leading manufacturers in the U.S.A. received invitation from Pan American Airways to submit bids for planes capable of carrying 100 passengers, with full stateroom, dressing room, and dining room accommodations, for a range of 5,000 miles, at a cruising speed of 200 miles an hour.
+ Colonel Alexander de Seversky, Russian-born aircraft designer and manufacturer, established an international non-stop record from Havana to Washington in four hours and fifty-one minutes. His average speed was 255 mph.
+ The first airmail flight across the U.S.A., made by Galbraith and Rogers in 1913, took fifty days and sixty-eight stops.
+ When regular airplane service was established between San Francisco, California, and Auckland, New Zealand, the flying boats would cover the distance in four days, compared with nineteen for the swiftest steamships.

The longest article in one issue was a review of the Pan American Airways network of 50,000 miles in 1937 and a preview of 1938. One highlight would be the test flying soon of the world's largest airliner, the forty-three-ton Boeing 314 Atlantic Clipper. One issue of the club newspaper carried a song to a march tempo, We're the Aviation Scouts of Canada by Ernest H. Dainty, which began with the stirring message that it wouldn't be very long before the Aviation Scouts of Canada would be one million strong. War intervened.

In early August of 1938 four excited teenage boys – Norman

Dawber, Harold Scandrett, Ross Smyth and Jim Templeton – were announced as winners of a contest sponsored by the Aviation Scouts of Canada. They assembled in the offices of the Toronto Star to embark on the greatest thrill of their lives.

As there was no air service on the route, the four boys accompanied by Captain Boyd were driven to Buffalo where they boarded a luxurious twenty-one-passenger Douglas DC-3 of American Airlines. They landed at Newark's airport serving New York one hour and thirty-eight minutes later, much faster than a twelve-hour train ride. As one of the boys later wrote for Canadian consumption in his school magazine:

> On the plane we were served a delicious meal consisting of chicken sandwiches, salad, coffee and ice cream, served by the lovely stewardess. Air travel is a beautiful experience, but as for excitement, it is rather disappointing. Dizziness is almost impossible because looking out of a transport plane is just like sitting in your own easy-chair.

The next morning Captain Boyd introduced the four lads to Douglas "Wrong Way" Corrigan. Corrigan had become famous only a month before for taking off from New York supposedly for California but ending up in Dublin, Ireland, twenty-eight hours and thirteen minutes later. His plane was a nine-year-old single-engine Curtiss Robin. The aviation scouts found him very unassuming, modest and witty. Only a few days before, New York had been decked in green for the famous Broadway ticker-tape parade to recognize the Irish American's accomplishment.

Captain Boyd, representing the Toronto Star, earlier had a special invitation to talk to Corrigan before his steamer from overseas docked.

"Harry Connor, who was navigator for Howard Hughes on his round the world flight, told me that the reverse course to Dublin would have taken you over Atlanta, Georgia, and then to Mexico," Boyd said to Corrigan. "What do you have to say about that?"

Everybody laughed as Corrigan looked up and answered, "Not with my compass."

For many years the thirty-one-year-old Corrigan had been an

admirer of Lindbergh ever since he had helped to build the Spirit of St. Louis in the Ryan factory in San Diego. Prior to his Atlantic flight, he was employed as an electric welder at the Northrop company.

Corrigan had bought his used plane for $900 in 1936 and put nearly every dime he earned into it. A mechanic friend who helped him said Corrigan pulled out the original ninety hp OX-5 motor, traded some stuff for two used Wright engines, and put the best parts of each into the power plant which hauled him over the ocean.

The authorities did not look favourably on unapproved flights, especially after the disappearance and expensive search for Amelia Earhart in the previous year. Since he did not have the required authorization, Corrigan stuck with his story of compass error with an Irish smile and twinkle in his eyes. Nobody believed him. Most newspapermen left after a Corrigan interview with replicas of the Corrigan grin, and as they went away, one of them said: "That guy makes you grin with him until you feel silly."

Erroll Boyd took the boys up the 102 stories of the Empire State Building, then the world's tallest. The evening was spent at the Pennsylvania Hotel where the boys met Kay Kyser, famous orchestra leader, and his singer, Ginny Simms, later a Hollywood star who played opposite Cary Grant in Night and Day, the story of Cole Porter. Miss Simms even invited the older boys for a dance!

After a luncheon honouring Corrigan, Boyd accompanied the boys to one of the world's great amusement parks, Coney Island, where they rode on all the thrilling rides. Strange as it may seem, the only casualty with an upset stomach was Norm Dawber who later led a meritorious RCAF career as a pilot in World War II, winning the Distinguished Flying Cross.

The four boys split up to take the various trips that were part of their prizes. Dawber flew from New York to Los Angeles, where he met famous Hollywood actor Wallace Beery and climbed through a Douglas DC-4 transport to get an insight into what the future held. Jim Templeton took the more northerly route to San Francisco and back.

Ross Smyth flew Eastern Air Lines to Miami where he witnessed Pan American Airways clipper ships arriving from South America, four Boeing B-17 Flying Fortresses coming in from Columbia and the landing of the Boeing B-15, the world's largest military plane. Before winning the trip Smyth had organized a squadron of young boys in

Toronto in the Flying Aces Club sponsored by Flying Aces magazine. Captain Boyd accompanied the youngest winner, thirteen-year-old Harold Scandrett, on the four hour flight to Bermuda on the Pan American flying boat, Bermuda Clipper. They returned to New York on the Imperial Airways flying boat, Cavalier.

Back in New York the boys went to Floyd Bennett and Roosevelt Fields, inspected Corrigan's Curtiss Robin, and met famous designer Major Alexander P. de Seversky. Seversky, inventor of the first all-metal high speed fighter, had been an air ace with czarist Russia in World War I. Earlier in the trip Boyd had introduced the lads to Roger Q. Williams, pilot of the first U.S.A. to Rome flight in 1929.

The four members of Aviation Scouts of Canada enjoyed the most wonderful experience in their life, and expressed their gratitude that an influential man of Captain Boyd's experience and knowledge would devote so much time in helping and motivating a younger generation.

28

Recruiting Pilots for World War II

JUST PRIOR to the outbreak of World War II in 1939, Erroll Boyd decided to move to the United States and to apply for U.S. citizenship to enhance his employment opportunities from West Cornwall, Connecticut. He was also doing some flight instruction from a small airport at nearby Canaan.

Captain Boyd and his family were staying at the home of his very good friend, Major M.K. Lee, in West Cornwall. Lee was a flier in the First World War and had flown with most well-known pilots in the U.S.A. His home was a haven for fliers and his visitors included Frank Hawks, Ruth Elder, Bernt Balchen and George Haldeman. Airplane trophies were all over his house and the walls were decorated with photographs of famous ships and the pilots who flew them. Only the door from the famous *Columbia* was preserved from the hangar fire in 1934, and it was preserved in Lee's beautiful country home.

When Canada but not the U.S.A. entered the Second World War in 1939 Boyd reconsidered his decision and wished to return home to help in either a civilian or military capacity. He made a major but unsuccessful effort. C.D. Howe, then Minister of Transport and later boss of Canada's war effort, replied about a misunderstanding as to his position with regards to appointments in the civil aviation branch and in Trans-Canada Air Lines. He said the civil service commission and the airline were responsible for their own appointments and suggested that Captain Boyd, in view of his distinguished war record, write the defence department.

The Minister of National Defence, Norman Rogers, replied that it would be necessary for Boyd to be resident in Canada in order that his application might be considered. Since very few appointments were being made to the RCAF, the minister hesitated to suggest that Boyd return to Canada for the purpose of filing his application.

Determined to help Canada and Britain, Boyd finally found a way, serving as executive officer of the semi-secret Clayton Knight Committee working out of New York through 1940 and 1941. Towards the end of this period it became known as the Canadian Aviation Bureau.

The purpose of the Clayton Knight Committee was to interest experienced pilots in helping Canada and Britain in the war effort. This was very sensitive work requiring extensive communication to obtain volunteers while, at the same time, respecting the neutrality law of the United States.

Boyd's main job was to look for experienced American fliers who wanted to enlist in the RCAF or RAF, or wanted to fly in the transatlantic or British ferry services. This involved extensive travel throughout the U.S.A. setting up sub-offices and screening thousands of potential candidates.

The Knight Committee probably owed its origin to Canada's famous fighter ace of World War One, Air Marshall W.A. "Billy" Bishop, victor over seventy-two enemy aircraft. Bishop recalled that a large number of Americans had come to Canada in 1917 to enlist in the Royal Flying Corps and he felt certain that history would repeat itself. Right after the outbreak of the war, Bishop telephoned his American friend, Clayton Knight, who was attending the Cleveland air races at the time. Knight expressed interest and said he would contact some of his friends.

Knight, a native of Rochester, N.Y., was born in the same year as Erroll Boyd, 1891. He formed the committee in 1940 because he sensed correctly that World War II soon would involve the U.S. Knight had served in the first war with distinction in France as an American pilot in the Royal Flying Corps No.206 Squadron. He was shot down and wounded in 1918 and became a prisoner of war.

By January 1940, Bishop had been appointed the RCAF's director of recruiting. When Knight needed the assistance of an experienced administrator for his committee, Bishop singled out another First World War acquaintance, Homer Smith, who had inherited a family fortune and had been living in New York and Palm Beach. It was Smith who served with Boyd at the outbreak of the First World War in 1914 in the Queen's Own Regiment and had introduced Erroll to Evelyn Carbery, later to become Mrs. Boyd.

Homer Smith initially was opposed to the committee trying to conceal its activities and boldly decided to set up its headquarters in the prestigious Waldorf Astoria Hotel with subsidiary offices in many other cities. He called upon his old friend Erroll to assist him and to do much of the work. At this time Erroll had been acting as assistant to Roger Q. Williams in test piloting for Vincent Burnelli, known for his lifting-body designed aircraft. The new task would not be easy.

Before more action was taken by the Knight Committee, L.C. Christie, Canadian ambassador in Washington, conveyed a message to Prime Minister Mackenzie King from the "highest quarter" that U.S. authorities would not be embarrassed by U.S. citizens proceeding to Canada to enlist. On the other hand, one State Department official later quoted from the Neutrality Act that enlisting a person in the services of a belligerent could produce a fine up to $2,000 and imprisonment up to three years! There seemed to be two currents of thought in the U.S.A. at the time.

By the summer of 1940 the British Commonwealth Air Training Plan was facing a serious shortage of trained pilots. A little later, however, learning that solicitation of pilots was becoming embarrassing to the U.S.A., Canada considered disbanding organized efforts, but refrained upon learning that the State Department had acted independently of the White House.

At one point the State Department protested that Knight and Smith had been "damn careless" and "should slow down and pull in their horns." The department nevertheless responded to the many complaints from isolationists and anti-British elements with a meaningless bureaucratic answer. While there was no thought of investigating the Knight Committee, it was considered wise to get rid of some of its files and it later was renamed the Canadian Aviation Bureau.

After the U.S.A. entered World War II, Clayton Knight became combat historian for the Eighth and Twentieth Air Forces in the Pacific. A skilled artist, his magnificent drawing of the Japanese surrender – made while perched high up in the battleship Missouri – was one of the most dramatic recordings of that historic event. While a special correspondent for Associated Press he also sketched Air Marshall Harris of the RAF bomber command in his secret headquarters.

Knight's neighbour in West Redding, Conn., Elmo Roper of Roper Poll renown, described him as a war hero, artist, author, world traveller and early flying enthusiast. About his committee work, Roper wrote in 1956 that the venture involved more risk than most people realized because technically it was illegal at the time, and most of the committee members had to risk a turning of sentiment in the U.S.A.

Because of the unofficial nature of the committee's work, official statistics are rare if available at all, although scattered press clippings from different cities in the U.S. indicate the extent of Boyd's travels and the involvement of thousands of pilots. A press report in 1960 shortly before Boyd's death revealed he was instrumental in approving more than 200 American pilots for the ferry command service and, in addition, directed more than 500 other Americans to Canada to train for Canadian or British air service.

The British government certainly appreciated the committee's work because the Order of the British Empire later was bestowed upon Clayton Knight for his committee's work during the beginning of World War II. Lord Beaverbrook, the UK's minister for aircraft production and a native of New Brunswick, had a definite interest in the Clayton Knight Committee.

In order to not upset isolationist sentiment in the U.S., the Clayton Knight Committee did not advertise, but did obtain much free publicity. Press reports of Boyd's travels throughout the U.S., however, outlined in news stories such conditions for volunteers as education, flight experience, health and rate of pay for entry into the RCAF and RAF. Ferry pilots within England were sought to release others for combat duty. Ferrying across the Atlantic was the highest paid category at a minimum of $1,000 per month but required instrument rating and some airline experience.

News stories indicated that interview centres were set up in New York, Chicago, St. Louis, Oakland, Dallas, Kansas City and other major cities. Captain Boyd said emphatically that the Clayton Knight Committee would not consider any pilot employed by an airline company unless the company released the candidate.

"We are definitely not recruiting," Knight had declared. "We merely are interviewing candidates, giving them physical and flight tests, and then recommending them to Canadian authorities."

American laws prohibited the enlistment or enrolment in the U.S. for the armed forces of a belligerent nation. Pilots interested in the RCAF usually paid their own way to a border point such as Detroit.

One press report said that since the Clayton Knight Committee had been organized a year earlier, 10,000 applicants had been interviewed and 900 had been found acceptable. The committee was described as a volunteer American information group working in collaboration with the British government.

A report from New York in August 1940 said pilots engaged to shuttle warplanes from factories in the British Isles to military centres were being sent abroad by boat at the rate of twenty-five to thirty a week. One report from St. Louis in the summer of 1941 said about a dozen young men were leaving St. Louis each week to join the RCAF. The Knight Committee had estimated that 125 from the St. Louis area had already joined the British and Canadian aviation services. Four had lost their lives.

A St. Louis instructor on leave from Rivers, Manitoba, said there were eighty-six aviation schools in Canada providing all kinds of flight training. He estimated that about one tenth of the RCAF members were U.S. citizens.

One of the men recruited by Erroll Boyd to work in Chicago for the committee was pioneer pilot Frank Coffyn, who was taught to fly at Dayton, Ohio, by Orville Wright in 1910. Coffyn was a member of the original Wright brothers' exhibition team, and was the first to fly under the Brooklyn and Manhattan bridges. He designed and used the first aluminum pontoons, and took the first successful motion pictures from an airplane. Coffyn was a former president of the Early Birds. Among the many pilots Boyd personally "recruited" were racing and test pilot Earl Ortman and World War I pilot William H. Alexander who made the first New York to Bermuda hydroplane flight in 1930. Another was Colonel Joseph C. Mackey, founder of Mackey Airlines of Fort Lauderdale and pilot of the plane in which Sir Frederick Banting, co-discover of insulin, was killed in Newfoundland in 1941.

By December 7, 1941 – the bombing of Pearl Harbor – over 6,000 Americans were serving in the RCAF alone, more than six per cent of its strength. With U.S. entry into the war the Clayton Knight Committee was discontinued, and Erroll Boyd could take satisfaction from a task well performed. Boyd had become a naturalized American citizen before the U.S. district court at Hartford, Connecticut, on March 28, 1941, and was listed as being employed by the RAF Ferry Command.

29

Problems in New Orleans

REJECTED for U.S. military service because of his age, Boyd joined Higgins Industries in New Orleans, first as test pilot, chief test pilot, and then senior supervisor of flight inspection. His friend Guiseppe Bellanca initially was selected to head the company's aviation department, but did not stay there very long.

Higgins Industries was a huge defence contractor presided over by a dominant president, Andrew Jackson Higgins. It was described in its own publication as the world's largest builder of boats, and originators and patentees of the Higgins Eureka Landing Boats.

Higgins Industries was not known to many aviation buffs because its main business was in the marine field building plywood PT boats. It entered aviation due to the requirements of the war, but its achievements in aircraft production were minimal. A specialist in wood construction, it had no previous airplane-building experience, which would prove to be a great handicap.

In 1942 Higgins had received the third government contract for the building of an additional 1,200 twin-engined Curtiss-Wright Caravan C-76s, mainly of wood construction because of a presumed metal shortage. The Curtiss-Wright Company had unwisely accepted the challenge of the C-76, a venture destined to end in futility.

With expert wood-workers long departed, Curtiss-Wright had to sub-contract extensively. The first test flight of the C-76 in January 1943 proved the aircraft unstable, tail-heavy and structurally weak – and costs spiralled. A test aircraft broke up in mid-air in May, and the contract was cancelled early in August. Only twenty-five airframes had been completed, twenty at Louisville, five at St. Louis and none at Higgins.

Higgins' major contribution then became an order for 1,200 of the Curtiss Commando C-46, described as the largest twin-motored, all-metal cargo plane in the world. Its wing span equalled that of the Boeing B-17 Flying Fortress. About double the size of the ubiquitous DC-3 or military C-47, the C-46 was to be built under licence from the Curtiss-Wright corporation whose main aircraft manufacturing plant was in Buffalo where Boyd had tested Jennies in 1917. Higgins would also make wings for Curtiss-Wright.

The Curtiss Commando had evolved from the pre-war design of the CW-20, an all-metal thirty-six passenger airliner. With a gross weight more than the Boeing B-17 bomber, the CW-20 was first flown by Eddie Allen in 1940, followed by a quick military order by the army for its military equivalent known as the C-46. More than 2,000 were built at various plants around the U.S.A., but Higgins had managed only to complete two aircraft when their contract was terminated after V-E day, May 7, 1945.

While the Curtiss Commando was over-shadowed by the smaller, more reliable DC-3 and C-47, it enjoyed its finest hours during the war years over the treacherous Himalayas on the "hump" operation supplying Allied forces in China from bases in India. In the postwar era it found its niche as a cargo carrier. The once great Curtiss-Wright Corporation left the aircraft manufacturing business shortly after the war.

Unfortunately for Boyd, who loved to be near flying and aircraft, Higgins had received its contract at a time when Curtiss-Wright was beginning its decline. Curtiss-Wright's origins went back to the birth of aviation, and the long legal feud between the Wright brothers and Glenn Curtiss over patent rights. It is ironic that the merger of Curtiss and Wright in 1929 was organized by investment bankers. It became the world's biggest aircraft and engine producer and grew in corporate size by 1942 to be second only to General Motors. In spite of war profits, its short-sighted management did not plan effectively for the post-war boom in commercial aviation or for the coming of the jet age.

The November 1943 issue of Higgins' internal publication reported that Captain Erroll Boyd was in charge of the first demonstration of a Commando, presumably from Buffalo. At least

2,000 people had braved the elements to get a look at the big plane Higgins was to build in quantity.

The slow progress in building the metal airliner must have been frustrating to Boyd. While working with this company, Erroll became seriously ill in March 1944 and entered the hospital to have his right kidney removed. During his illness, Boyd received a termination notice from the aircraft division and was struck off the payroll for twelve weeks. He had difficulty paying his medical bills and house rental on time.

While still under the doctor's care, Boyd was able to work later in the summer. He appealed his status to the company president, Andrew Higgins, in mid-July and eventually was given a reassignment. Erroll's daughter, Honor, also worked for Higgins in an office capacity before joining TWA as a stewardess in 1946.

30

From Warrior to Man of Peace

ERROLL BOYD entered the First World War like most young men—as a gung-ho warrior eager to become a military hero. His journey through life witnessed a transition to a man of peace. By 1938 this man of vision was advocating a peace air force for the League of Nations, the predecessor of the United Nations—an idea still valid and awaiting implementation.

In Boyd's vision, every nation desirous of cooperating towards universal peace would subscribe to an international air pact and pledge to maintain a portion of its air force ready for mobilization at short notice. These combined forces would be at the permanent disposition of the League of Nations, although each would be maintained in its own country during time of peace.

This force would be under the command of an air marshall named by the league, supported by a general staff and air vice-marshals from major contributing countries. The force would function in two ways.

First, in the event of pronounced tensions between two countries, it would be directed by the league to fly over the borders and cities serving as a pacific police force, thus indicating the power at the disposal of the league and its ability to enforce its mandate for peace. It might drop peace propaganda among the peoples of the disputing territories. It might provide aid in the event of natural disasters, of which there are about fifty per year.

Second, in the event that a demonstration of power by the league was not effective, the united peace force would be mobilized to assist that party to be considered in the right by the league and to block off commercial or other communication between the offending country and the outside world – a powerful deterrent in itself.

Boyd's ideas for the "silver wings of peace" was not completely original. A similar plan had been suggested in the late 1920s by Clifford Harmon, sponsor of the Harmon Trophy for famous aviators. Boyd felt that its earlier implementation could have prevented the cruel war between China and Japan and the civil war in Spain and that its existence would be a logical follow-up to the Kellogg-Briand anti-war pact of 1928. This international treaty to abolish war was initiated by the foreign ministers of the U.S.A. and France, but became ineffective as it lacked the means of enforcement.

Boyd later reminisced and questioned the purpose of war as a method of settling disputes. Possibly he had more in common with the enemy pilots than with the diplomats and politicians. He once wrote:

> There are two sides to war – yours and mine . . . A hostile aircraft flies over our city and drops bombs . . . Wounded patients, innocent civilians, helpless women and children are slaughtered. The damning agony of suspense of a night attack leaves invisible scars.
>
> How can I stop it? Supposing these men who were hired to murder me and my family were invited to my apartment. We would discuss problems of life and death. Possibly we would agree on the futility of killing each other. But this would get us nowhere. We and they are not important enough to count. The fate of the world is not hanging upon our shoulders. We are merely patriotic killers.
>
> On the other hand, supposing I invited into the same apartment a group of diplomats. We become very familiar. Yet I know and they would know that anything we said or did would be a lie. These men are trained in a profession to fabricate the truth in the same way and with the same precision that I am trained to kill in the air and on the ground . . . These gentlemen flatter me and remain my friends only so long as I execute their murderous demands. So long as the war lasts, either I continue to follow in accordance with their political plans, or else . . .
>
> I might have these charming gentlemen as guests –

but I would feel far safer with the men against whom I shall be forced to combat . . . Why did these diplomats and patriotic murderers decide in 1914 that I should go out and kill according to their dictates any man, woman or child whose fate threw them in my way? Why should I hazard my life in effecting the schemes of these self-ordered gods of war?

I did not ask these questions in 1915. I was young. I thought I was about to become a hero.

The ideas of Captain Erroll Boyd about war are consistent with human welfare and the aims of the peace movement. Is it not time now to revive the proposal for a Peace Air Force under the command of the United Nations?

31

The Post-War Years

FOLLOWING World War II, with some of their daughters married, Evelyn and Erroll Boyd developed a pattern of spending their winters in Florida and summers in Cornwall, Connecticut, with frequent visits to Toronto.

In 1946 the Boyds' youngest daughter, eighteen-year-old Virginia, known as Jini, earned the title of Miss Miami Beach of 1946. Their second youngest daughter, Honor, was working as a stewardess with TWA during 1946-48. Their eldest daughter, Bey, suffered two tragedies: her first husband was killed in a bombing mission in a Wellington over Germany in 1941, and her second husband, also a pilot, was killed in an automobile accident near Barrie, Ontario, in 1949. The Boyd's second eldest daughter, Kathleen, assisted her dad in his return to the hotel business after the war.

Bruce Knight, Bey's first son and Erroll's oldest grandchild, recalls a winter visit to Florida when he supplemented family income with an extensive newspaper route. He recalls his grandfather as a fun-loving, friendly, generous man who loved entertaining and partying – but, outside of his family, he loved flying the most.

"Erroll even would talk about aviation to the local merchants and trades people, and often take them aloft to experience the thrill and enjoyment of their first flight," Bruce recalled.

Based on his earlier experience in New York in the 1920s, Erroll regained employment in hotel management, especially during Florida's busy winter season. For example, in 1947 he leased and operated the Devon Hotel on Indian Creek Drive in Miami Beach.

Two of his early guests at the hotel were Major J. Nelson Kelly, former managing director of Roosevelt and Floyd Bennett fields in New York, and P.H. Spencer, plane designer. Kelly arrived in his new Seabee designed by Spencer. The Seabee was a very flexible amphibian with a 500-mile range, very useful for hunting and fishing.

"The plane is fine for a honeymoon," according to Boyd, an old friend of Kelly's. "It has sleeping accommodation for two people."

Erroll Boyd continued to fly intermittently through to 1957 and accumulated more than 9,000 hours of flying time. In all his forty-two years of flying he wore a parachute on only one occasion.

"The only time I had a parachute on my back," he said, "was when I buried Bob Lyons' ashes in 1940 – then only because the U.S. Navy made it compulsory."

Boyd lost a friend with the death of colourful pioneer pilot Bert Acosta. Writing from a TB sanatorium in Denver, Colorado, in late 1954, Acosta reminisced: "How well I remember the old days training the Canadians at the old rifle ranges near Sunnyside, Toronto, and having a hell of a good time, and the real satisfaction of a job well done."

In early 1953, the year marking the fiftieth anniversary of the first flight by the Wright brothers, the *Miami Daily News* carried a story that twelve 'greybeards' were planning a round-the-world hop and that famed pilots of the past were "rarin' to go."

"We've seen a great deal of the world," Boyd said, "but we'd like to see more before we're too old." Boyd was sixty-one. Captain Cloyd Clevenger, aged fifty-six, would be probably the youngest on the flight. He had thirty-five years of flying with thirty-two transatlantic ferry trips under his belt.

The Greybeards, a name coined by Associated Press, were the survivors of the early pilots who had pioneered the application of airplanes to commercial pursuits. Their flights with fragile and inadequate equipment had focused attention on the unlimited possibilities of flight. Their activities had stimulated inventive and manufacturing genius to develop better planes, engines and instruments.

With very few exceptions these pioneers did not profit financially from their exploits. Of the human qualities that produced their feats of daring, business sense at a young age was usually not one of them. The ability to foresee the financial possibilities of their flights and to capitalize on them was conspicuous by its absence. Their reward may have been some glory and the short-lived acclaim of an admiring public, while others reaped the profits.

Yet they sought no charity. Through their own efforts, they would acquire a suitable plane and make a profitable, farewell flight around the world to create a fund to be administered by competent trustees to supplement their pension income.

Every legitimate source of revenue – such as advertising, stamps, covers, photographs, autographs, movies, radio and television – would be explored to make it a success. Such was the purpose of the proposed Greybeards' farewell flight as often discussed by Erroll Boyd and Cloyd Clevenger over a friendly drink shortly following World War II.

The plans for the Greybeard flight moved very slowly due to political turbulence in Korea and in many parts of the world, but accelerated as the fiftieth anniversary of flight approached in 1953. The two were joined by Boyd's friend, Frederick E. "Ted" King of New York, who was qualified to handle the administrative and legal work.

Ted King, a corporate lawyer, founder of the Wings Club, and legal advisor to the Quiet Birdmen, was a World War I navy flier who had been associated with the planning of the navy's transatlantic NC-4 flight in 1919. He had been commander of the NC-2 which did not complete the crossing.

Cloyd Clevenger, an early barnstormer who had become a living legend in Mexico, was at the time a transport pilot for the Dominican Aviation Company. As a young flying instructor he had given lessons to businessman Harry Knight who, as president of the St. Louis Flying Club, had played a key role in financing Charles Lindbergh's *Spirit of St. Louis* flight in 1927.

Such famed pilots as Clyde Pangborn, George Halderman, Clayton Knight, Jimmy Mattern, Bernt Balchen, Roberto Fierro, Dick Merrill, Walter Hinton, Sir Hubert Wilkins and Frank Coffyn were interested or being considered, in addition to publicists such as Lowell Thomas.

It was initially proposed to take ten passengers at $5,000 a head, and make some exotic stopovers. It was felt that Shell would sponsor the fuel.

The aircraft proposed for the flight was a modified war surplus Boeing B-17. After a fund-raising tour of the U.S.A., it would commence its round-the-world trip in the Dominican Republic to promote the construction of El Faro de Colon, The Lighthouse of Columbus, a monument to which the great explorer's remains would be moved when finished.

With an estimated twenty million postage stamp collectors in the U.S.A. alone, Boyd had received considerable interest from stamp dealers. Clevenger had lobbied top government leaders in the Dominican Government who expressed great interest in the project. An affirmative response, however, was always delayed in coming down from the big boss, General Trujillo (who would be assassinated in 1961).

Even when 1953 passed without success, Clevenger, still actively flying throughout the Caribbean, persisted in keeping the idea of the project alive, and at one time thought he had the financial backing of President Somoza of Nicaragua. The flight, however, never materialized.

32

The Perfect Landing Field

IN 1955 the Boyds managed, after much searching, to purchase a beautiful retirement home, described as a 'perfect landing field' and one of the most picturesque spots in all Florida. Located on the Hillsboro Shores of Pompano Beach, Erroll and Evie Boyd continued to prove they were wonderful hosts. The welcome mat was always available to their relatives and friends. Evelyn was also active in the North Broward Society of the Symphony.

The four Boyd daughters and their families will never forget the happy memories of joining their parents and friends where Erroll played the piano and they all sang along with the ever popular songs. They were a musical family.

All members of the Boyd family were very air-minded. Youngest daughter Virginia Semenenko, wife of Serge Semenenko, an affluent Boston banker, had already made thirty-eight airline trips to Paris. In 1955 she helped her mother achieve a lifelong dream by taking Evelyn Boyd on a three-month trip abroad.

In Pompano Beach Erroll's pride and joy was his study, a miniature museum with mementoes of great moments in the history of aviation. One wall was devoted to that most famous plane of its era, the Bellanca *Columbia*. This study was the centre for his research and work on a book which unfortunately was not quite completed before his death in 1960.

Boyd in later life attended many reunions of pioneer pilots. For example, he attended a meeting of the OX-5 Club in Miami on the thirtieth anniversary of Lindbergh's flight to Paris. This club consisted of pilots who flew aircraft in the early 1900s powered by the

Curtiss OX-5 engine such as the Jenny. A local paper reported on Boyd's attendance, noting that "Boyd, whose son-in-law, Boston banker Serge Semenenko, recently bought Warner Bros. Studios for $68,000,000, was one of the first pilots to fly the famous Jenny during World War I as a test pilot for his native Canada."

During the latter years of his life Erroll suffered many health setbacks. Early in 1957 he suffered a stroke while on a visit to Toronto, and spent nine weeks there in Sunnybrook Hospital. This was followed by a vascular accident in September involving his left arm and leg. As a result of further deterioration, the left leg was amputated in May 1958 to prevent gangrene.

Late in life Boyd's wife Evelyn was forced to learn to drive due to her husband's illness and, while not a pilot, she could be described as a flying grandmother. On one occasion a policeman stopped her for speeding.

"What's the matter, lovey?" she asked the startled cop.

"You're going eighty-five miles an hour," he said.

"Was I?" she asked sweetly.

Boyd, Charles Levine, Cloyd Clevenger at 1959 reunion, Pompano Beach, Florida (Courtesy of Boyd family)

On the basis that she was visiting her ill husband in the hospital, she managed to escape without a fine.

In 1959 Erroll was quite ill with recurrent intestinal hemorrhage. When he first moved to Pompano Beach, he had weighed 217 pounds, but his weight had fallen to 128, then climbed back up to 155.

During all this illness, the pioneer airman's indomitable courage and optimism prevailed. In an interview in July 1960, a few weeks after his second stroke, he commented with a grin: "The doctors had almost given me up for dead. They thought I was a goner, but I fooled them." He wanted to stay alive to see his book published.

During this period he still did a little travelling, entertained many friends and made a valiant effort to complete his book. One of his visitors in 1959 was his navigator Harry Connor whom he had not seen in many years.

In reporting on this pioneer aviator reunion, the *Miami Herald* recalled their famous 1930 transatlantic flight. Boyd mentioned being sworn in as a postman, and reminisced: "Blocks of four stamps that went with us on the envelopes now sell for around $7,000".

Boyd said their flight to Bermuda four months earlier was considered one of the finest navigation feats in flying records. Without radio, finding Bermuda in the wastes of the Atlantic was like looking for a needle in a haystack, he said.

"As long as Connor could stick his head out of the back of the plane and take readings of the sun or the stars, there was no danger of getting lost," Boyd said in tribute to his friend. This achievement led to Connor's selection by Howard Hughes as navigator for the 1938 round-the-world record flight in a Lockheed 14, made in three days and nineteen hours, cutting more than half the time off Wiley Post's 1933 flight.

Connor revealed that, before his 1930 flights with Boyd, he had practised pinpointing ocean liners some 400 miles out to sea, and that such practice had helped him to improve greatly his navigating ability by the time of the Bermuda flight.

During the late 1950s Boyd addressed a group of his peers on flying the Atlantic in the good old days. The report of it read:

> His comments were extremely interesting and his talk
> was greatly enlivened when several five-inch Fourth of
> July "salutes" were unexpectedly fired off. Erroll later

entertained us on the piano and didn't even miss a beat when another "salute" exploded directly beneath his "Francis." That bird sure has nerves of iron!

In 1959 famed commentator Lowell Thomas invited Erroll Boyd to New York to participate in the thirty-fifth anniversary of the first circumnavigation of the globe by air by the U.S. Army fliers in 1924. Erroll was unable to accept, presumably due to his health. Six survivors of that flight would be present with former president Hoover chairing the event.

In a Miami paper renowned columnist Walter Winchell mentioned that Erroll Boyd was writing a book at Pompano Beach. In another column, Boyd was described as a real 'old pro' aviator working on his forthcoming book, *Dead Stick Landing*:

> In his den, Pierre, a coal-black four year old French poodle, "stands guard" while his master once again goes through file after file on the famous plane and its exploits.
> With one leg recently amputated and other stomach and internal disorders cropping up regularly, the Captain shuttles quietly around his den in a wheelchair, arranging papers, making telephone calls, and "always planning ahead." He has no time for regrets or reminiscences.

Gwen Harrison of the *Miami Herald* wrote in September 1959, in her column under the caption "Wheel chair goes on trip with Boyds" that Erroll Boyd had approval from his doctor for a fast trip north of not more than ten days – and that a trip to New York never fails to please his wife, the former Evelyn Carberry, "the prettiest of grandmothers," since Manhattan was the scene of her show business successes. Mrs. Boyd did the driving.

The Boyds stopped over in Cooperstown, New York, to visit briefly with their long time friend, pioneer pilot Viola Gentry. Evelyn and Viola visited the Baseball Hall of Fame there, but Erroll's lack of mobility prevented his visit. Viola, a friend of Amelia Earhart, had just completed a book on her flying experiences. At this time Boyd was considering retitling his book, *Miss Columbia, Queen of the Air*.

The Boyds drove on to Toronto to visit their eldest daughter Bey and her three children and Erroll's sister, Dorothy (Mrs. Ernest

Macrae) at Milton. On their return they stopped over in New York to visit friends and see Erroll's proposed publisher. They undoubtedly overstayed the doctor's time limitations!

Visitors to the Boyd residence in the summer of 1960 included Charles Levine and Cloyd Clevenger. Although the controversial Levine had spent time in prison for shady business dealings and had been termed the Mad Mullah of aviation, Erroll Boyd never made very critical comments about Charlie, who had provided the plane for his epic transatlantic flight. Found in his files many years later were the following notes: "Levine good guy and crackpot to let me do it – lending me plane without security to make a transatlantic flight."

A report in the Florida press in 1960 mentioned that a well known aviation writer from New York, Martin Caidin, would assist Captain Boyd with the completion of the manuscript of his book. The report also mentioned that, during his remarkable career, Erroll Boyd had close dealings with such well known figures as John D. Rockefeller Sr., Will Rogers, Wiley Post, Charles A. Lindbergh, Jimmy Doolittle, Claire Chenault, Amelia Earhart, Howard Hughes, Eddie Rickenbacker, Tallullah Bankhead, Pat O'Brien, James A. Farley, Jimmy Roosevelt, Robert Taylor and many others.

The Boyds were at their summer home in West Cornwall, Connecticut, later in the summer of 1960 when Erroll's health deteriorated further. After a lengthy illness he died in the nearby hospital at Sharon on November 27, shortly after his sixty-ninth birthday. He was buried in Florida near Evelyn's residence at Pompano Beach.

Erroll Boyd had lived from the birth of aviation to the dawn of the jet age. He not only witnessed great changes but was an active participant in bringing them about. He saw the airplane develop from a flimsy and dangerous contraption into a vehicle of mass transportation that was beginning to reshape the world into a global village.

By being one of the first Canadian fliers in the Great War in 1915, he served his country well. Much more than a warrior, he was really a man of peace. In the 1930s he supported the idea of a peace air force and held the vision that expanded air travel could unite the world. With Hitler's invasions, however, he rallied to support the cause of defending freedom. Considered too old for active duty, he recruited ferry pilots in the then neutral U.S.A.

He pioneered new routes and instrument flying before the era of modern instruments. While pilots of his era were often labelled as reckless devil-may-care stunt pilots, he was a relatively cautious flyer who loved life too much to take unnecessary risks.

Erroll was an optimist and a dreamer, albeit a practical dreamer. He foresaw the great future in aviation, one that was slowed somewhat by the Great Depression of the thirties. His predictions nevertheless were remarkably accurate. Even when in financial difficulty, he took time out to encourage and help youth to enter this new field.

He was a man ahead of his time, which created difficulties in gaining employment at what he liked doing best – flying. Today's airline pilots can fly regularly up to age sixty or sixty-five, and there are even some flight instructors in their eighties. In the inter-war period, however, being over forty was considered by most as too old for piloting.

Erroll Boyd was an intelligent, talented man who could have achieved success in almost any field to which he devoted his energy and enthusiasm. But he chose flying. His father was undoubtedly disappointed that he had not selected and stayed with a more stable and traditional business, but Erroll once said that "flying gets a hold of you and you can't keep away from it."

Boyd was a quintessential Canadian. He loved Canada and reflected the Scottish background of his father and the United Empire Loyalist and Irish adventuresome tradition from his mother's side. He was pulled to the United States through love, marriage and big city life. At times this could be either an advantage or a disadvantage.

Just before his death Boyd wrote on a photo to his daughter, Bey: "Here's to a life of high adventure." But she insisted correctly that his life was devoted to furthering and developing aviation.

History increasingly will highlight his achievements, particularly the first transatlantic flight by a Canadian in 1930, and the very first by anyone outside the summer season. Erroll Boyd was a member of that small group of early pilots that played a pioneering role in making North America number one in air transport, and that in turn contributed to the growth of aviation worldwide. And Erroll was a very loveable and decent human being.

Index